WILLIAM HAZLITT
AND THE MALTHUSIAN
CONTROVERSY

WILLIAM HAZLITT AND THE MALTHUSIAN CONTROVERSY

WILLIAM P. ALBRECHT

KENNIKAT PRESS
Port Washington, N. Y./London

WILLIAM HAZLITT AND THE
MALTHUSIAN CONTROVERSY

First published 1950
Reissued in 1969 by Kennikat Press
Library of Congress Catalog Card No: 70-85980
SBN 8046-0597-1

Manufactured by Taylor Publishing Company   Dallas, Texas

PREFACE

Modern geneticists consider unsound Malthus' assertions regarding the pressure of populations upon potentials of subsistence. They are of course *ad hoc* assertions, for he had no statistics, nor did he hazard statistical prediction to bolster his argument. Yet it sounds plausible, so much so that there still are propagandists either so unprincipled or mistaken as to deserve being called neo-Malthusian. These persons argue, for example, that sending food to Asia merely fosters a larger population and in consequence greater misery. Nothing, we now know, could be further from the truth. In actual fact countries having the highest standards of living begin leveling off soonest in rate of increase of population. Although but indicative figures concerning population in the Far East can be reached, there is no doubt that its rate of increase is greater than that of England or the United States. In short, raising living standards brings in its train decrease in rate of addition to population until stability, even decline, set in. Strange as it may sound then, the Occident should worry more about too few citizens than too many. Technological skill and improvement of marginal land, as well as contraception, are among the developments causing standards of living in the United States, for instance, to outstrip pressure of population. And conversely, as has been said, the misery and dearth of the East have not checked its growth in numbers as they would have if Malthus' theory were sound. The conclusion from these observable facts is that Malthus, in addition to his relationships with such literary opponents as Godwin and Hazlitt, is significant as a phenomenon in history and political science. Frequently the mistakes of history, or those who make them, loom more significantly across the page than do the 'right' thinkers of lesser contemporary influence. A case in point is Milton, whose stature as a literary figure contrasts with his having been negligible politically. Wordsworth may have been right in the famous sonnet addressed to him that England had need of his spiritual strength and humility in 1802, but the fact nevertheless remains that his "soul was like a Star, and dwelt apart." Over against such a literary illustration is Malthus' theory,

3

which should now be a dead issue and is so looked upon by
biologists, but which played a significant part in English political issues of the Napoleonic period. Parliamentarians like
Whitbread, who fathered the Poor Law, found in Malthus
basis for their rationalizations, and the well-to-do were glad
to find in a comfortable doctrine sanction for things as they
were. In this sense Malthus answered a 'need' of his time. Because he did, a study of the controversies in which he was em-
broiled is of real importance historically. More important still,
the agricultural and industrial conflicts of the day; the attitudes of Tory, radical, and Whig; such events as the Corpo-
ration and Speenhamland Acts (the latter using wheat as a
commodity index, the former forbidding collective action)—
all these are immediately apprehendable as once-living issues in
the pages of Hazlitt and Malthus. Clearly, too, Hazlitt's literary stature gives continuing interest to what he said in the
controversy.

The sinewy force of Hazlitt's polemical style has been obscured by the attention so deservedly paid to his critical and
conversational styles of writing. As the present volume points
out, he could develop an organized argument when he cared
to. (Witness his tightly-reasoned *Principles of Human Action,*
in which his idea of 'imagination,' arising out of eighteenth-
century empirical psychology, means 'the ability to apply the
effects of experience to forseeable acts of the future.') Yet his
interest in social questions ran so deep that he was not above
becoming the propagandist and using personal vilification in
pursuit of what he considered worthwhile ends. This, I should
think, would hardly surprise any one familiar with Hazlitt's
robust attitudes. He deserves, what is more, to be put with the
strongest polemical writers in English and at his best equals
Junius, whom he admired. To take but one illustration: both
Junius and Hazlitt adapted the eighteenth-century periodic
style to their modes of attack, making it a most gratifying in-
strument to those who relish invective. What it lacks in subtlety,
it makes up for in sharpness and surprise, for antithesis and
balance are often employed to mislead the reader, who is then
darted in upon with a condemnation. Hazlitt's most sustained
performance in this kind is *A Reply to Z* (William Gifford),

certainly one of the most astounding vituperations ever set down. The *Reply* to Malthus is of course only interlarded with passages of personal ridicule, but their saltiness makes the argument more palatable.

Dr. Albrecht's study also re-emphasizes Hazlitt's preoccupation with the fate of the poor and lowly. Like Byron, he gave himself to liberty without yielding to the psychology of the 'herd.' He was an intellectual democrat. His aberration regarding Napoleon or his opposition to Robert Owen's scheme of social improvement sprang from the same deep-seated desire as his opposition to Malthus: the love of liberty. He was as honest as he was intense, often prejudiced, often wrong. And he almost never changed an opinion once he formed it. But he is, like Dr. Johnson, so frequently illuminating when he is wrong, or so inevitably right when he is right that he will continue to be read when 'sounder' men have been forgotten.

STEWART C. WILCOX

Norman, Oklahoma
December 30, 1949

ACKNOWLEDGEMENTS

For suggestions regarding the subject and the method of this study I am grateful to Professors Ronald S. Crane, Clarence H. Faust, Carl H. Grabo, and Robert Morss Lovett, all—at that time—of the University of Chicago. Also I wish to thank the editors of *Modern Language Notes* and the University of Pittsburgh Press, respectively, for permission to republish herein portions of my articles "Hazlitt and Malthus," *Modern Language Notes* (April, 1945), and "Hazlitt's *Principles of Human Action* and the Improvement of Society," *If By Your Art: Testament to Percival Hunt* (Pittsburgh, 1948). Above all I am grateful to my wife for her share in this project.

WILLIAM P. ALBRECHT

Albuquerque
November 7, 1949

TABLE OF CONTENTS

WILLIAM HAZLITT AND THE MALTHUSIAN CONTROVERSY

INTRODUCTION

As the eighteenth century came to an end and the nineteenth began, the rights of Englishmen were suffering curtailment—both in practice and in theory. The excesses of the French revolution had gone far toward discrediting the doctrine of the rights of man and, together with hard times, had made the ruling class in England and even the other classes fearful of revolt. With bad harvests at home, high taxes, trade disrupted by war, and, after 1815, the collapse of markets, distress among the poor became more than usually severe; and in fear of violence, the rights of the working class were narrowly circumscribed. Pitt suspended the Habeas Corpus in 1794, and in 1795 Parliament passed two bills prohibiting public meetings. Societies of working men were suppressed, and their leaders prosecuted; and by the Combination Laws passed in 1799 and 1800, workmen were prohibited from taking any common action in defense of their interests. When, during the hard times after the war, laborers rioted for bread, the work of suppression was carried on with increasing harshness. An act of 1817 suspended the Habeas Corpus, and in the same year three other coercion acts were passed by great majorities.

Acute poverty gave force to the theory that the right to subsistence is not society's responsibility but is "naturally" limited to what a laborer can earn in "free" competition in the labor market. To political economists, therefore, rational "self-love" appeared to be a more useful motive than "benevolence"; and if the ruling classes considered benevolence socially useful, it was likely to be in contenting the working classes with poor-relief. The conception of benevolence as a moral obligation, revealed by reason, to grant the rights of others persisted in Godwin, Owen, and other radicals, but their writings had little practical effect in relieving poverty: Owen's proposed Villages of Co-operation, although safely within the

9

laws of property, were rejected by the Committee of the House
of Commons on the Poor Laws, partly because they ran coun-
ter to the theories of political economy and partly because
Owen had criticized the established system of property and
wages.[1]

On account of disgust with "wild speculations" of revolutionary thought, Southey wrote in 1803, the "moral and political atmosphere" had become "unnatural and unwhole-
some";[2] and, according to Shelley in 1817, "gloom and misan-
thropy" were still "characteristic of the age . . . ."[3]

William Hazlitt shared the current skepticism of a society
of "perfectly" rational and moral beings, but he continually
defended the rights of man. He objected particularly to what
he considered the narrow psychology and the low aims of
political economy; for, he believed, the insistence that economic improvement depended on rational self-interest free
from governmental interference was, practically, a denial of
human rights and was, moreover, inimical to any improvement
whatsoever. Hazlitt's explanation of human behavior limits
society's approach to "perfection," but even a lesser degree of
improvement, Hazlitt thought, could be realized only through
increased virtue and benevolence.

For Hazlitt, therefore, the *Essay on Population* by Thomas
Robert Malthus became a symbol of all that was antithetical
to improvement. In his *Reply to the Essay on Population* and
throughout his political essays the name of Malthus stands
for oppression: for all the tyranny and selfishness that, Hazlitt thought, robbed the laboring class of freedom and sub-
merged it in hopeless poverty. This identification, as Hazlitt
half admits, is not a just one, and the theory of the *Essay,*
Hazlitt acknowledges at times, is not to be refuted; but because the principle of population, or frequently some perversion of it, was cited by Malthus and others in support of meas-

---

[1] Robert Owen, *The Life of Robert Owen by Himself* (New York: Alfred A.
Knopf, 1920), p. 215; G. D. H. Cole, *The Life of Robert Owen* (2d ed.; London:
Macmillan and Company, 1930), pp. 20-30.

[2] [Robert Southey], "Malthus's Essays on Population," *Annual Review*, II
(1803), 292.

[3] Preface to *Laon and Cythna, The Complete Works of Percy Bysshe Shelley,*
ed. Roger Ingpen and Walter E. Peck (London: Ernest Benn Limited, 1927-30),
I, 241-42.

ures that Hazlitt thought would depress the poor still further, he attacks the author and the principle, as well as the application, in order to destroy the prestige of Malthus's sanction. From 1807, then, when Hazlitt's first attack appeared anonymously in Cobbett's *Weekly Political Register,* until the last years of his life, Malthus was the frequent victim of Hazlitt's indignation.

Hazlitt's *Reply to the Essay on Population* was published anonymously in 1807.[4] Comprising five "letters," of which the first three appeared originally in the *Weekly Political Register,*[5] and a series of "Extracts" from the *Essay* accompanied by "a commentary," it must be considered a long reply even among the wordy pamphlets of the Malthusian controversy. In 1819 the second and third letters, changed only slightly, were published a third time, together with part of the "Extracts," in Hazlitt's *Political Essays.*[6] In 1810, following a comment on the *Reply* in the *Edinburgh Review,*[7] Hazlitt replied with a letter printed in the *Weekly Political Register,* republished five years later in *The Examiner,* and finally included among the *Political Essays.*[8] A fifth *Political Essay* on population, which is a summary of the fourth letter of the *Reply,* had previously appeared in both *The Morning Chronicle* and *The Yellow Dwarf;*[9] and in "Mr. Malthus" in *The Spirit of the*

---

[4] William Hazlitt, *A Reply to the Essay on Population by the Reverend T. R. Malthus, The Complete Works of William Hazlitt,* ed. P. P. Howe (London: J. M. Dent and Sons, Ltd., 1930-34), I, 177-364. Further references will be to this edition of Hazlitt's *Works.*

[5] "Poor Laws," *Weekly Political Register,* IX (March 14, 1807); "Poor Laws. Being the Second Letter of A. O.," *Weekly Political Register,* XI (May 16, 1807); "Poor Laws. Being the Third Letter of A. O.," *Weekly Political Register,* XI (May 23, 1807).

[6] "On the Originality of Mr. Malthus's Essay," "On the Principle of Population as Affecting the Schemes of Utopian Improvement," and "On the Application of Mr. Malthus's Principle to the Poor Laws," *Political Essays, Works,* VII, 337-43, 343-50, 350-57.

[7] "Disquisitions on Population," *Edinburgh Review,* XVI (August, 1810), 464-76.

[8] "Queries Relating to the Essay on Population," *Political Essays,* pp. 357-61. "From the *Political Register,* November 24, 1810. Reproduced by Hazlitt in *The Examiner,* October 29, 1815, as No. 23 of the Round Table series." (Editor's note, *Political Essays,* p. 408.) The opening of the letter is printed in the Notes to the *Political Essays,* pp. 408-10.

[9] "An Examination of Mr. Malthus's Doctrines. I. Of the Geometrical and Arithmetical Series," *Political Essays,* pp. 332-37. Published with slight differences in "*The Morning Chronicle,* September 2, 1817, unsigned, entitled 'Mr. Owen and Mr. Malthus.' Also published in *The Yellow Dwarf,* April 4, 1818,

Age (1825)[10] Hazlitt once more repeats the arguments that run through the *Reply* and the *Political Essays*. The frequency with which Hazlitt, in the essays that I have mentioned and in many shorter passages as well, repeats his case against Malthus suggests his continued interest in the *Essay on Population,* the importance that he attached to its influence, and his own evaluation of the *Reply.* He thought well enough of his arguments not only to repeat them frequently but to defend their originality at least twice.[11] Furthermore, in a note to one of the *Political Essays* he mentions the style of the *Reply* as "a little exuberant" but "see[s] no reason to be ashamed [of the arguments]";[12] and in his "Project for a New Theory of Civil and Criminal Legislation," which was begun in 1792 but revised presumably about 1825 or 1826, Hazlitt again expresses his satisfaction with the *Reply.*[13]

Comment on Hazlitt's *Reply*—and any comment on the *Reply* is applicable to his other essays on population—has been slight, but on the whole more favorable than unfavorable. According to James Grahame in 1816, "the anonymous author of the Reply, &c. has commented at great length, and with a great deal of acuteness, on Mr. Malthus' comparison of the increase of population to a geometrical series."[14] J. A. Field credits Hazlitt with "interesting as well as earl[y] . . . contributions to the theory of prudential restraint. . . ."[15] In his *Life of William Hazlitt,* P. P. Howe points out that Hazlitt "tackled [the *Essay*], as it required to be tackled, with

---

signed 'W. Hazlitt,' with the present title and subtitle." (Editor's note, *Political Essays,* p. 407.)

[10] "Mr. Malthus," *The Spirit of the Age, Works,* XI, 103-14.

[11] Letter to Leigh Hunt, April 21, 1821, quoted in Ford K. Brown, *The Life of William Godwin* (London: J. M. Dent & Sons Ltd., 1926), p. 334, n. Cf. also letter published in the *London Magazine* for November, 1823, quoted in Thomas DeQuincey, "Malthus on Population," *The Collected Writings of Thomas De Quincey,* ed. David Masson (London: A. & C. Black, 1897), IX, 20-22.

[12] "On the Application of Mr. Malthus's Principle to the Poor Laws," *op. cit.,* p. 350, n.

[13] "Project for a New Theory of Civil and Criminal Legislation," *Literary and Political Criticism, Works,* XIX, 309. Cf. Editor's note, p. 367.

[14] James Grahame, *An Inquiry into the Principle of Population* . . . (Edinburgh: Archibald Constable and Co.; London: Longman, Hurst, Rees, Orme, and Brown, 1816), p. 72.

[15] James Alfred Field, "The Malthusian Controversy in England," *Essays on Population and Other Papers,* ed. Helen Fisher Hohman (Chicago: The University of Chicago Press, 1931), p. 41.

spirit."[16] According to Ford K. Brown in *The Life of William Godwin,* "Hazlitt's refutation appears overwhelming" to "the modern student who sees that Malthus was far from correct in predicting an immediate danger. . . ."[17] "Hazlitt loses his temper," Crane Brinton admits in *The Political Ideas of the English Romanticists,* "and often overshoots his mark," but he "writes soundly on the wage-fund theory of Malthus" and "expose[s] the great Malthusian fallacy that an improved standard of living among the poor must in itself cause an increased birth rate and a relapse into misery."[18] In the *Encyclopaedia of the Social Sciences* Hazlitt's *Reply,* "although [called] intemperate and sometimes unfair," is recognized as "a serious contribution to the Malthusian controversy."[19] A more detailed, and certainly favorable, treatment of the *Reply* is Catherine Macdonald Maclean's in *Born Under Saturn.* The *Reply,* Miss Maclean points out, is directed against the practical effects of the *Essay,* rather than Malthus's speculation, and against the "vulgar selfishness" which the *Essay* seemed to typify and encourage. Seeking an "understanding of [Hazlitt's] character" in the *Reply,* she shows that it was Hazlitt's devoton to liberty that led him to oppose Malthus; but with "Malthus's theories as such" she has "no concern," nor does she mention Hazlitt's countertheories.[20]

On the other hand, the *Edinburgh* reviewer in 1810 attributes to the author of the *Reply* "strange misapprehensions and misrepresentations of the doctrines [he] profess[es] to discuss . . . ."[21] De Quincey "read [the *Reply*] cursorily" with-

16 P. P. Howe, *The Life of William Hazlitt* (New York: Richard R. Smith, Inc., 1930), p. 100. Cf. pp. 364-65.

17 *Op. cit.,* p. 333.

18 Crane Brinton, *The Political Ideas of the English Romanticists* (London: Oxford University Press, 1926), p. 133.

19 Alfred Cobban, "William Hazlitt," *Encyclopaedia of the Social Sciences,* ed. Edwin R. A. Seligman and Alvin Johnson, VII (1932), 286.

20 Catherine Macdonald Maclean, *Born under Saturn* (New York: The Macmillan Company, 1944), pp. 225-32.

21 "Disquisitions on Population," *op. cit.,* p. 465. "As the relations of Malthus to the *Review* were close at this time, and as the arguments and the style are remarkably like our author's, there is at least a strong probability that he wrote [this] article, Jeffrey after his custom providing it with a head and tail to disguise the authorship." (James Bonar, *Malthus and His Work* [2d ed.; London: George Allen and Unwin Ltd., 1924], p. 329, n.) If Jeffrey wrote the beginning of the review, the passage quoted above is his.

out discovering what Hazlitt later asserted to be his important arguments, and testifies "to hear[ing on several occasions] this book of Mr. Hazlitt's treated as unworthy of his talents . . . ."[22] James Bonar, who has written the standard work on Malthus, dismisses Hazlitt as one of the critics who "say the doctrine of the essay is a truism."[23] Norman E. Himes, in the introduction to his edition of Francis Place's *Illustrations and Proofs of the Principle of Population,* speaks disparagingly of the length of the *Reply* but attempts no further evaluation.[24]

All of these comments are short. With the exception of the review in 1810, De Quincey's essay, and Miss Maclean's analysis, none of them comprises more than two or three pages, and most of them consist of only a few sentences more than the portions I have quoted. Undoubtedly the length of the *Reply,* its repetitions, its contumely, its apparently wilful misrepresentations of Malthus's argument have caused it often to be ignored or underestimated. But when the *Reply* is considered in relation to contemporary events, the misrepresentations and even the contumely are often explained, if not justified, by the current misconceptions of Malthus's position and Hazlitt's interest in the effect of the *Essay* on the poor rather than in the principle of population itself. My examination of the *Reply,* therefore, and Hazlitt's other essays on population could be justified as restoring the background necessary for understanding some of the less important works of an important writer; but interest in these essays may be derived from more than their authorship. Despite the abuse and the misrepresentations, Hazlitt seems to have grasped more fully than most of the contemporary critics what later writers on population agree to be the valid implications of the *Essay,* and at the same time he suggests the adaptation of Malthus's doctrine that has been made to account for more recent population phenomena.

In anthologies of English literature Hazlitt is likely to be represented by "On Going on a Journey," "My First Acquaint-

---

22 *Op. cit.,* pp. 25-26.
23 *Op. cit.,* p. 394. Cf. pp. 85, 372, and Dr. Bonar's Foreword to Field, *op. cit.,* p. viii.
24 Francis Place, *Illustrations and Proofs of the Principle of Population.* . . . , ed. Norman E. Himes (Boston: Houghton Mifflin Company, 1930), Introduction, p. 23. Cf. pp. 35, 57-58.

ance with Poets," "The Fight," and possibly one piece of
literary criticism. His accomplishment in the literature of ideas
is too often overlooked or depreciated. One anthology even
states that after 1807 Hazlitt was "resigned to his failure as
a philosopher" and "turned to general critical writing . . . ."[25]
Hazlitt had little capacity for resignation, and I doubt that he
ever thought himself a failure as a philosopher—at least if
philosophy is considered, as it was in Hazlitt's time, to deal
with problems of human thought, motivation, and behavior.
That his treatment of these problems in relation to economics
and politics was not altogether unsuccessful is shown by his
writings in the Malthusian controversy.

Because Hazlitt's attack is directed primarily against the
application of the *Essay* to the treatment of the poor, and because it is often a perversion of Malthus's argument that was
used against measures for relieving poverty, it is necessary, in
order to explain and evaluate the *Reply,* to see that Hazlitt is
diverted from Malthus's more valid arguments at least partly
because some absurd inferences drawn from them seemed likely
to, and apparently did, affect legislation. It is necessary, moreover, to isolate his attack on the false inferences in order to
see wherein and how effectively he meets Malthus's own arguments. To point out, therefore, the "tyrannical" applications
that Hazlitt objected to, the arguments used in their support,
and which of these arguments were sanctioned by Malthus, and
to discover as well to what extent Hazlitt repeats the stock
arguments of the controversy and how far he goes beyond
them, I have examined, especially for the years 1798 to 1821,
(1) measures proposed or adopted for dealing with poverty,
(2) the different editions of the *Essay,* (3) literature defending the principle of population and urging its application, and
(4) several other replies to Malthus.

The years 1798-1821 have been chosen for several reasons.
Field divides the Malthusian controversy into three periods:
1798-1821, 1822-1834, and 1835-1870—the first part "coex-
tensive with the influence of Godwin and of the war" and
"characterized as the period of refutation and bold accept-

---

[25] George B. Woods, Homer A. Watt, and George K. Anderson, *The Literature of England* (3d ed.; Chicago: Scott, Foresman and Company, 1948), II, 360.

ance," the second part "transitional" and "marked by . . . the reform of the poor laws[,] . . . the death of Malthus," and propaganda for contraception, and the third part contributing "the scholastics of population theory."[26] Hazlitt's attack on Malthus, although his "Mr. Malthus" in *The Spirit of the Age* and other essays containing allusions to the *Essay* were published after 1821, unquestionably belongs to the first period, both in time and in thought. Most of Hazlitt's essays on population were published before 1821 and all of them repeat, frequently verbatim, arguments from the *Reply*. Although Hazlitt's attacks on Malthus after 1821 sometimes refer to contemporary events, the issues are still derived from the Godwin-Malthus controversy and the emphasis is still that of the *Reply*.

My first chapter contrasts Godwin and Malthus, for since Godwin's *Political Justice* and *Enquirer* provoked the *Essay,* an understanding of his position is necessary to an understanding of Malthus. Moreover, the dispute between Godwin and Malthus established the dominant issues of the 1798-1821 period, especially as far as Hazlitt is concerned, and suggested the basic argument of the *Reply.* In the second chapter, I have shown how the *Essay* was accepted or rejected among different political groups as sanctioning or repudiating their policies with regard to improvement, and how during the years 1798 to 1821, political expediency brought Malthus's doctrines into still greater favor. The third chapter is an analysis of the first three letters of the *Reply* with special attention to the explanation of human behavior underlying them, Hazlitt's political position, and the rhetorical method used in the *Reply.* The fourth chapter compares Hazlitt's with Malthus's treatment of the arithmetical and geometrical ratios. The fifth chapter gives Hazlitt's case against human institutions as the cause of suffering, and the sixth his defense of the Poor Laws. Chapter seven deals with Malthus on institutions. Chapter eight relates Hazlitt's essays to more recent population phenomena and theory, especially with regard to the prudential check, and closes with a brief re-statement of Hazlitt's position in the controversy.

---

[26] *Op. cit.,* pp. 77-80.

As far as I know, the early replies to Malthus have not heretofore been analyzed in relation to the political situation responsible for them. Field and Bonar discuss Malthus's critics, but rather briefly and with little reference to the political thought and events of the time; and although Himes brings out enough of the background of the Malthus-Godwin dispute to explain Francis Place's contribution, he does not pay much attention to the other critics. Summaries of the controversy in histories of economic thought or in books on population can only suggest the political conflict. There are, of course, other aspects of the controversy—such as the religious and ethical ones and the influence of earlier economic theory on the replies—that, in a complete history of any period of the controversy, should be brought out more fully than I have attempted here; but since the critic's politics seems usually to have determined his position in the controversy, a study of the political issues is especially useful for an understanding not only of Hazlitt's *Reply* but also of most of the early objections to the *Essay*.

Chapter I

GODWIN AND MALTHUS

When Malthus in the first edition of the *Essay* proposed a middle course between the conservatism of those who wished to preserve the political and economic status quo and the radicalism of those who were working for great changes in society,[1] he indicated the three main lines that the early reaction to the *Essay* was to follow: for while Malthus's fellow Whigs gladly accepted his middle course, both the Tories and the Radicals, for different reasons of course, attacked the principle of population as false and pernicious. The radical reaction was at least a partial defense of the doctrines of William Godwin, whose *Enquirer* had provoked the *Essay*[2] and against whose *Political Justice* the *Essay* was mainly directed. The Whigs and the Tories, on the other hand, were united in their attack on Godwin, and when the Tories finally joined the Whigs in supporting the *Essay,* it was partly from a fear of Godwin's ideas. For these reasons, and because Godwin himself contributed two replies to Malthus, an analysis of his *Political Justice* is essential to this study.

Godwin's Society of Disinterested Citizens and Economic Equality

In political literature the opposition of "reason" to "passion" and "benevolence" to "self-love" assumed—in Godwin's *Political Justice* and Malthus's *Essay*—two contradistinguishing patterns. Combining the doctrines of "utility," "necessity," and the rights of man, Godwin finds promise of rational and moral behavior and, therefore, of complete political and economic equality. Just as experience relates cause and effect in the material world, Godwin argues in *Political Justice,* so does it bind them together by necessity in the mind itself, linking with certain propositions "the notions of preferableness or the

---

[1] Thomas Robert Malthus, *First Essay on Population, 1798* (London: Macmillan & Co., Ltd., 1926), pp. 3-5.
[2] *Ibid.,* Preface, p. i.

contrary" and directing, thereby, one's tendency to action.[3]
Now, since "men always act upon their apprehensions of
preferableness," their actions will be virtuous and just—that is,
making for the general happiness—if by connecting cause
and effect they can see the preferableness of such actions. But
a higher law than any made by man is on the side of justice.
The "immutabl[e] tru[th] that whatever tends to produce a
balance of [happiness and pleasure] is to be desired, and
whatever tends to a balance of [misery and pain] is to be
rejected" is "founded in the nature of things," for "vicious
conduct is soon discovered to involve injurious consequences."
If, therefore, man is allowed the free use of his reason—the
faculty that enables him to foresee consequences—he cannot
but act toward increasing the general happiness.[4]

Therefore, men have no "rights" in the sense that they may
or may not choose a certain line of conduct, for justice demands
that they act always to increase the general happiness; but since
it is every man's duty to employ himself to this end as best he
may, everyone possesses, as the correlative of his neighbors'
duties, certain negative rights.[5] That is to say, as Godwin adds
in his second edition, "every man has a right to that, the
exclusive possession of which being awarded to him, a greater
sum of benefit or pleasure will result, than could have arisen
from its being otherwise appropriated."[6] A quantity of food,
clothing, and shelter necessary to keep a man alive will
obviously contribute more to the general happiness by being
awarded to a man who is entirely without food, clothing, or
shelter than by being granted to one who is already adequately
supplied with such property. Therefore, if the division of both
labor and produce were made according to the demands of
justice, everyone would have enough material goods at the cost
of perhaps only half an hour's work per day.[7] Everyone would
have the leisure necessary to further mental development, and

---

3 William Godwin, *An Enquiry Concerning Political Justice* . . . (London:
G. G. and J. Robinson, 1793), I, 286-90, 343-45, and *passim*. Godwin acknowledges his debt to Hume. (*Ibid.*, p. 296, n.)
4 *Ibid.*, I, 31, 75, 121-22, 346 ff.; II, 830-31, and *passim*.
5 *Ibid.*, I, 110-12.
6 *An Enquiry Concerning Political Justice* . . . (2d ed. corrected; London:
G. G. and J. Robinson, 1796), II, 415-16.
7 *Political Justice* (1st ed.), II, 790-92, 823.

consequently greater virtue, and would enjoy to a higher and still higher degree the intellectual pleasures which give man his greatest happiness.

For progress toward such a society, truth must be made known through freedom of inquiry and freedom of expression.[8] Government must not perpetuate vice by preserving the distinction between rich and poor, for if a common stock of goods were built up through the labors of every citizen, "temptation would lose its power."[9] Along with private property, Godwin condemns such other "erroneous institutions" as marriage, religious conformity, oaths of fidelity, and laws for the suppression of libel. From all of these, government should withdraw its sanction and confine itself to the suppression of unjustice against individuals and defense against invasion. As truths become more general and men more just, even the first of these will become hardly necessary and the latter not a matter of maintaining a regular army but of a virtuous citizenry rallying to defend the common interest.[10]

Thus, according to Godwin, reason may dominate passion, and, as it does, concern for the benefit of the whole will replace selfishness in directing action. The rational man, when confronted with two alternatives, will choose that tending to the greater increase of general happiness.

MALTHUS'S CRITICISM OF THIS SOCIETY

Political economy also relied on the power of reason to connect cause and effect and to determine behavior accordingly; but as far as the production and distribution of goods was concerned, "self-love" rather than "benevolence" was designated as the socially useful motive.[11] Adam Smith as-

---

8 *Ibid.,* II, 878-93.

9 *Ibid.,* I, 34.

10 *Ibid.,* II, 564-67.

11 "Benevolence," as used by most contemporary writers, seems to denote an emotion, whereas "virtue" in *Political Justice* apparently involves only reason without emotional impetus. Later, however, in a memorandum intended "to correct certain errors" in *Political Justice,* Godwin acknowledges the need for emotion in directing voluntary actions, and limits the province of reason "to adjusting the comparison between different objects of desire, and investigating the most successful mode of attaining these objects . . . ." Virtuous action will spring from "a disposition naturally kind and well tempered," but it will be regulated by "general utility." (Quoted in Brown, *op. cit.,* pp. 135-36.)

sumed a natural or inherent principle whereby the good of all results from the self-seeking of each and laid down competitive effort for gain as the basis of the economic system, inferring that a wise government should leave prices and wages to the law of supply and demand, and charity to the discrimination of individuals.[12] "Benevolence," narrowed in meaning to the public or even private support of the poor, was deprecated as interfering with free competition and therefore as being "unjust."

Malthus, replying to Godwin by elaborating a proposition from *The Wealth of Nations*,[13] stresses the resistance of passion to reason as well as the social efficacy of self-love. Nature, according to the *Essay on Population*, instead of making for a communistic anarchy of disinterested citizens, insures the division into economic classes, with self-love as the ruling principle. Because the sexual passion is "necessary" and "constant" and because the food supply is limited—ultimately by the earth's productivity and actually by many intervening factors—population will always increase to a point where, regardless of human institutions, a marginal group must suffer want.

Although "ardently wish[ing] for such happy improvements" as Godwin predicts,[14] Malthus finds that the "fixed laws of our nature" sharply limit our progress toward perfection. Two of these "laws" are expressed as the postulates basic to the whole argument of the *Essay*: "First, That food is necessary to the existence of man," and "Secondly, That the passion between the sexes is necessary, and will remain nearly in its present state." Malthus argues that "these two laws ever since we have had any knowledge of mankind, appear to have been fixed laws of our nature, and, as we have not hitherto seen any alteration in them, we have no right to conclude that they will ever cease to be what they are now," except through the intervention of God.[15] Assuming his postulates granted, Malthus continued by pointing out "that the

---

12 Adam Smith, *An Inquiry into the Nature and Causes of the Wealth of Nations*, ed. Edwin Cannan (London: Methuen & Co., 1904), I, 142-44.
13 "The demand for those who live by wages, it is evident, cannot increase but in proportion to the increase of the funds which are destined for the payment of wages." (*Ibid.*, I, 70-71. Cf. *First Essay*, p. 8.)
14 *First Essay*, p. 7.
15 *Ibid.*, pp. 11-12.

power of population is indefinitely greater than the power in the earth to produce subsistence for man." As observable in the United States of America, population when unchecked by lack of subsistence "increases in a geometrical ratio," whereas for "the average state of the earth" food production "could not possibly be made to increase faster than in an arithmetical ratio."[16] Therefore, since "by that law of our nature which makes food necessary to the life of man, the effects of these two unequal powers must be kept equal," there must be "a strong and constantly operating check on population from the difficulty of subsistence."[17]

This check may be either "positive" or "preventive." The positive check "represses an increase which is already begun," often killing off redundant population by means of undernourishment, strenuous labor, and other hardships accompanying poverty.[18] But man, after all, is a "compound being," possessing not only "instinct" and "physical propensities" but also "Reason, that faculty which enables us to calculate consequences. . . ."[19] Although he is "impelled to the increase of his species by an equally powerful instinct, reason interrupts his career, and asks him whether he may not bring beings into the world, for whom he cannot provide the means of subsistence." In his first edition, however, Malthus does not separate the prudential check from vice and misery. Even though an increase is prevented, such "restraint almost necessarily . . . produces vice."[20] The word "vice," as Malthus later defines it, distinguishes "that class of actions, the general tendency of which is to produce misery, but which in their immediate or individual effects, may produce perhaps exactly the contrary."[21] The word "misery," which has troubled some critics by its vagueness, covers other forms of suffering than those resulting from lack of food, although Malthus, when he uses the word, generally has these latter forms in mind. He seems to have

---

16 *Ibid.*, pp. 13 ff.; T. R. Malthus, *An Essay on the Principle of Population* . . . ([2d ed.]; London: J. Johnson, 1803), Bk. I, chap. i, pp. 2-7.
17 *First Essay*, pp. 14-26.
18 *Ibid.*, pp. 71-73.
19 *Ibid.*, pp. 215-16.
20 *Ibid.*, pp. 27-29, 69-70.
21 *Essay* (2d ed.), Bk. I, chap. ii, pp. 11-12, n.

chosen it simply as a general term antithetical to the "happiness" that Godwin expected to be consummated in the future. ". . . Illicit intercourse between the sexes" is vicious, Malthus points out, because it leads to misery or, in other words, "tend[s] . . . to injure the happiness of society."[22] Primarily, then, "vice and misery" are introduced as conditions that would have to be got rid of in a society of complete morality and happiness.

Godwin's *Enquiry* concerns *Political Justice, and Its Influence on Morals and Happiness*. Malthus's thesis is that *vice* and *misery* exist at least partially outside the influence of government or the form of society and that, therefore, the influence of "political justice" on "*morals* and *happiness*" is less than Godwin supposes. The pressure of want on at least part of the population will always exist and will always be so great that some men will be led to encroach upon the possessions of others.[23] Malthus, however, does not content himself with finding Godwin's "justice" inconsistent with "nature." Equal distribution achieved through benevolence, he thinks, is unnatural; but self-love may work for the happiness of the group and bring about, if not the equitable distribution that would be deemed "just" among disinterested beings in a world of plenty, at least the approximation to it that must be considered "just" among selfish men in a world of limited resources. In a community such as that foreseen in *Political Justice*, where the communal stores were open to all, population would increase so rapidly that food production could not keep pace and scarcity would soon result. ". . . The spirit of benevolence" would be "repressed by the chilling breath of want," and "the mighty law of self-preservation" would soon restore "self-love" to its "wonted empire . . . ." "Vice" as well as "misery" would check population. Depredations from the common store would increase until "the laws of our nature" re-established, as the best remedies for overpopulation, private property and, so that every man would have to support his own children, marriage. A division into classes—proprietors and laborers—would then be inevitable, for those "born after the division of property"

22 *Ibid.*
23 *First Essay*, p. 267.

would have to work for those who had more than enough for themselves.[24]

To make the most of the protection against overpopulation provided by private property and marriage, Malthus urges the abolition of the Poor Laws and the education of the working class, so that the poor may discover their own responsibility for poverty. The prudential check, classified in the first edition of the *Essay* as a form of vice and misery, appears in the second edition, with certain modifications, as a separate check called "moral restraint." By moral restraint Malthus means the postponement of marriage until one is able to support a family which, for all one knows, may be a large one and the practice of "strict chastity" in the meantime.[25] Having detached this form of the prudential check from immoral consequences, Malthus puts more stress on the withdrawal of poor relief as a means of enforcing moral restraint. But since he does not foresee "any great change in the general conduct of men on this subject," he does not expect any great diminution of poverty.[26] To make the most of an inherently bad situation the capitalistic system is better than economic communism, and self-love is more useful than benevolence; but even with free and selfish enterprise, inequality and poverty must *naturally* continue.

---

[24] *Ibid.*, pp. 11-26, 185-206, and *passim.*
[25] *Essay* (2d ed.), Bk. IV, chap. ii, pp. 495-96.
[26] *Ibid.*, chap. iii, p. 504. Cf. *First Essay*, p. 277.

CHAPTER II

THE CONTROVERSY, 1798-1821

The *Essay* exerted great influence both in current thought and in practical politics. Despite the abuse of critics and the shower of "refutations," it went through six editions[1] in Malthus's lifetime, and Malthus almost immediately could claim such variously distinguished converts as Paley,[2] Parr,[3] Erasmus Darwin,[4] and Cobbett.[5]. The first part of the Malthusian controversy, 1798-1821, may be divided by the end of the war (1815) into two periods, each inaugurated by hard times and unrest, and marked by new proposals for solving the problem of poverty. When, in the closing years of the century, the growing discontent among the working classes and the turn taken by the French Revolution increased the fear of rebellion in England, Malthus's condemnation of sweeping changes in society readily found supporters. His proposed course between "the advocate for the present order of things" and "the advocate for the perfectibility of man and society"[6] appealed especially to the chastened liberalism of the Whigs: with its first number, in 1802, the *Edinburgh Review* began to champion the principle of population;[7] and in their attitude toward Poor-Law legislation, the Whig politicians Pitt,[8] Whitbread,[9]

---

[1] 1798, 1803, 1806, 1807, 1817, and 1826.

[2] William Paley, *Natural Theology* . . . (London: W. Mason and Baldwyn and Co., 1817), chap. xxvi, pp. 432-33. Cf. T. R. Malthus, *An Essay on the Principle of Population* . . . (5th ed.; London: John Murray, 1817), Vol. III, Bk. IV, chap. xiii, pp. 300-01, n.; and [William Empson], "The Life, Writings, and Character of Mr. Malthus," *Edinburgh Review*, LXIV (January, 1837), 483. (For the attribution to Empson see Brougham's letters in Macvey Napier [ed.], *Selections from the Correspondence of the Late Macvey Napier, Esq.* [London: Macmillan and Company, 1879], pp. 187-88.)

[3] Samuel Parr, *A Spital Sermon Preached upon Easter Tuesday, April 15, 1800, The Works of Samuel Parr . . . ,* ed. J. Johnstone (London: Longman, Rees, Orme, Browne, and Green, 1828), II, 593-94.

[4] Erasmus Darwin, *The Temple of Nature* (London: J. Johnson, 1803), Part IV, ll. 369-74.

[5] *Weekly Political Register*, VI (December 8, 1804), 864-87; VII (February 16, 1805), 230-31; IX (January 18, 1806), 65. Later Cobbett became one of Malthus's most bitter opponents.

[6] *First Essay*, pp. 3-5.

[7] "Dr. Parr's Spital Sermon" and "Godwin's Reply to Parr," *Edinburgh Review*, I (October, 1802), 18-24, 24-26.

[8] By 1800 Pitt had dropped his poor bill because of objection "by those whose

and Brougham,[10] were guided by Malthusian principles. But just as political and economic conditions gave an impetus to the acceptance of the *Essay,* the opposition to Malthus became most articulate at those times when, to many, the course of events in England seemed to corroborate his doctrines and demand their practical application. During 1798-1814 Radicals and Tories alike attacked Malthus: most of the replies and the first four editions of the *Essay,* with replies to some of the critics, appearing between 1798 and 1808. Then, as huge war profits compensated landlords and farmers for the cost of feeding the poor and as manufacturing demanded more and more cheap labor, the controversy quieted down—until, after the war, the foreign and domestic markets collapsed. With new hard times and new riots, Tory writers and politicians found wisdom in the doctrines of Malthus. In 1817 the *Quarterly Review,* after gradually modifying its opposition to the *Essay,* fell into line, and the Poor-Law Act of 1818, which was justified in Parliament on what were at least thought to be Malthusian grounds, won the support of both parties. At the same time a new series of replies and Malthus's fifth edition were published. Hazlitt's *Reply* (1807), which was provoked directly by Whitebread's Poor Bill, belongs to the first of these periods; the *Political Essays* (1819), to the second.

REACTION TO THE IDEAS OF THE FRENCH REVOLUTION

At the end of the century times were propitious for the acceptance of the *Essay*: the attack on Godwin was enforced by reaction to the ideas of the French Revolution, and the attack on the Poor Laws, to which Malthus shifted his emphasis in the second edition, was confirmed by the already es-

---

opinions he was bound to respect." (Hansard, *Parliamentary History,* XXXIV [1800], 1428-29.) The remainder of the passage suggests that Pitt was referring to Bentham and Malthus. Empson in "The Life, Writings, and Character of Mr. Malthus" (*op. cit.,* p. 483) wrote, "We have repeatedly heard him [Malthus] say that the two converts of whom he was most proud, were Dr. Paley and Mr. Pitt."

[9] Hansard, *Parliamentary Debates,* VIII (1807), 865-921.

[10] *Ibid.,* XXXIII (1816), 1115; 3d series, XXV (1834), 220. Cf. British Museum, Add. MS. 30121, fol. 256—cited by Arthur Aspinall, *Lord Brougham and the Whig Party* (Manchester: The University Press, 1927), p. 73.

tablished doctrines of political economy and given point by the failure of increasing poor rates to diminish poverty.

The excesses of the revolution in France had not only discredited change of almost any sort but, together with hard times for the poor at home, had made the ruling class in England and even the lower classes fear revolt. The demands of radical writers were not for confiscation and division of the great estates, but the landowners and tithe-owners "had seen tithes, and all seignorial dues abolished at almost a single stroke across the channel. . . ."[11] With the war against France and bad harvests in 1794, 1795, and 1800, the price of wheat rose sharply and as usual the poor were the sufferers.[12] These crises led on the one hand to proposals for relieving distress and on the other to repressive measures such as the suspension of Habeas Corpus, the prohibition of public meetings, and the Combination Laws.[13] "Infamous as [the Treasonable Practices Bill and the Seditious Meetings Bill] were," Francis Place testifies, "they were popular measures."

The people, ay, the mass of shopkeepers and working people, may be said to have approved them without understanding them. Such was their terror of the French Regicides and democrats, such was the fear that 'the throne and the altar' would be destroyed, and that we should be 'deprived of our holy religion,' that had the knowledge of the grand conspiracy been equal to their desires, they might have converted the Government into anything they wished for the advantage of themselves.[14]

This dread in itself must have been enough to win converts to the *Essay*, but since it was coupled with a fear of a growing population,[15] as a menace to the established order, the *Essay*

---

11 J. L. and Barbara Hammond, *The Village Labourer, 1760-1832* . . . (4th ed.; London: Longmans, Green, and Co. Ltd., 1927), p. 144.

12 *Ibid.*, pp. 82-98; J. L. and Barbara Hammond, *The Town Labourer, 1760-1832* . . . (London: Longmans, Green and Co., Ltd., 1928), pp. 95-98.

13 Hansard, *Parliamentary History,* XXXII (1795), 242-554; Graham Wallas, *The Life of Francis Place* (4th ed.; London: George Allen & Unwin Ltd., 1925), pp. 25-26 and *passim; The Town Labourer,* pp. 98, 112 ff.

14 Quoted in Wallas, *op. cit.,* p. 25, n.

15 The first census (1801) gave the population of England and Wales as 9,172,960, and earlier figures have been estimated as follows:

1714	5,750,000
1760	7,000,000
1780	8,000,000

Cf. Sir George Nicholls, *A History of the English Poor Law* (London: John

apparently appealed to certain classes both as sanctioning the status quo and at the same time discouraging the increase of population that threatened it. Gardner's attack on large population as facilitating "assemblage" and thus leading to "seditious turbulence, and secret conspiracies"[16] adds weight to Ensor's testimony that Malthus's doctrine was all the more acceptable because it "rush[ed] in with a flood of fearful opinion" and because "when the French people had exerted their power, a great population was easily proved a tremendous evil. . . ."[17]

Other critics point out the current disillusionment with schemes for "perfect" societies. With *Political Justice* evidently in mind, Southey traces the popularity of the *Essay* to disgust with such revolutionary thought as "wild speculations how men might live forever."[18] Shelley attributes the popular triumph of Malthus over Godwin, and the pessimism it symbolized, to loss of "hope in the progress of French liberty."[19] On the other hand, Malthus together with other political economists won the approval of the *Edinburgh Review* for "trying to benefit mankind not so much . . . by exhibiting for their choice perfect patterns of political constitutions" but simply "by enlightening those who administer the systems already established."[20]

THE PROBLEM OF POVERTY

In his second edition Malthus directed more attention to the Poor Laws and proposed a plan for their gradual abolition; but even in the first edition his opposition to poor relief,

---

Murray, 1854), Vol. II, Appendix I, p. 465; and J. R. McCulloch, *A Statistical Account of the British Empire* (London: C. Knight and Co., 1837), p. 406.

[16] Edward Gardner, *Reflections upon the Evil Effects of an Increasing Population* . . . (Gloucester: R. Raikes, 1800), pp. 14-15, 77-82.

[17] George Ensor, *An Inquiry Concerning the Population of Nations* . . . (London: Effingham Wilson, 1818), pp. 85-86.

[18] *Op. cit.*, p. 292. Cf. [Robert Southey], "Inquiry into the Poor Laws," *Quarterly Review*, VIII (December, 1812), 321-22. The attribution of these articles to Southey is based on J. W. Warter (ed.), *Selections from the Letters of Robert Southey* (London: Longman, Brown, Green, and Longmans, 1856), II, 304; C. C. Southey (ed.), *The Life and Correspondence of Robert Southey* (London: Longman, Brown, Green, and Longmans, 1850), II, 251, 294; VI, 399, 400; Robert Southey, *Essays, Moral and Political* (London: John Murray, 1832), pp. 75-247.

[19] *Op. cit.*, pp. 241-42.

[20] "Inquiry into the State of the Poor," *Edinburgh Review*, XI (October, 1807), 101.

although incidental to the attack on Godwin, was unequivocal. The Poor-Law system had been in effect since 1601, when the State had accepted the responsibility, taken over from the church, of caring for the poor. In each parish, overseers appointed by the justices of peace collected the poor rates, which were levied on owners of land and all those occupying it on any sort of title, and either the overseers themselves or parish guardians, also appointed by the justices of peace, administered relief to the needy residents of the parish. By the closing years of the eighteenth century, however, this system maintained the poor only in hardship and virtual slavery. Out relief, or a weekly allowance of a shilling or two at home, had gradually been curtailed in favor of indoor relief in workhouses or poorhouses, where men and women, adults and children, diseased and well were crowded together in often desperate and sometimes riotous squalor.[21] The Poor Laws, moreover, had become a system of employment as well as relief; and the able-bodied poor who could not find private employment might be employed directly on parish work or shared out among the rate payers, or the parish might sell their labor to the farmers at a low rate and pay part of their wages out of the poor fund.[22] The inadequacy of this system is apparent in contemporary reports on the condition of the poor,[23] in the discontent among the working class, and in the remedies suggested. In 1795 and again in 1800 Whitbread proposed fixing a minimum wage.[24] Pitt, although rejecting Whitbread's minimum-wage proposal, suggested supplementing wages out of the poor rates, with an added allowance increasing with the number of children.[25] Realizing the harm of enclosure acts in depriving the poor of their land and cows, Arthur Young and others pro-

---

[21] *The Village Labourer,* pp. 122-24. Cf. Sir Frederic Morton Eden, *The State of the Poor . . .* ,abridged and edited by A. G. L. Rogers (London: George Routledge & Sons, 1928), pp. xxxviii-xliv, 230, 240, 252, 285-86, 319, 372, and *passim.* Although Eden's reports suggest that in the later eighteenth century public opinion had forced an appreciably higher standard of comfort and sanitation in the workhouses, they also indicate the misery in which the poor were often forced to live. Cf. George Crabbe, *The Village,* Bk. I, ll. 228-346.

[22] *The Village Labourer,* p. 124; Nicholls, *op. cit.,* II, 14-18, 92-93.

[23] Eden, *op. cit.,* pp. 129 ff. and *passim.*

[24] Hansard, *Parliamentary History,* XXXII (1795-1796), 700-15; XXXIV (1800), 1426-30. Cf. Nicholls, *op. cit.,* II, 139.

[25] Hansard, *Parliamentary History,* XXXII (1796), 705-12, 1405. Cf. Nicholls, *op. cit.,* II, 125-29.

posed allotments of land to the poor.[26] Changes in diet were suggested.[27] But the only remedy put into effect on any appreciable scale was that of the magistrates who met in Speenhamland on May 6, 1795, with the avowed purpose of raising the wages of the laborer. The "Speenhamland Act" provided that the laborer's wage should be proportional to the price of wheat and that the difference between this normal wage and the wage actually paid must be made up out of the poor rates. This plan, usually with its weekly allowance of enough to buy three gallon loaves of bread for the laborer and one and one-half for his wife and for each child, was gradually adopted in county after county, so that throughout the greater part of England the agricultural laborer—deprived by enclosures of the land he had once used for farming and grazing and generally prevented by the Settlement Laws[28] from seeking higher wages in another parish—lost what freedom of bargaining had hitherto been left him and became dependent on the parish for a subsistence wage. Even the laborer in private employment had to accept what the farmer chose to pay and to receive the remainder of his allowance from the parish.[29]

This was the Poor-Law system that Malthus attacked. There is no remedy, according to the first edition of the *Essay,*

---

[26] Arthur Young, *The Question of Scarcity Plainly Stated and Remedies Considered* (London: W. J. and J. Richardson and J. Wright, 1800), pp. 25-26, 76-77, and *passim;* Arthur Young, *An Inquiry into the Propriety of Applying Wastes to the Better Maintenance and Support of the Poor* (Bury: Richardson and J. Hatchard, 1801).

[27] *The Question of Scarcity,* p. 69; Eden, *op. cit.,* pp. 100-07.

[28] The responsibility of the parish was limited to supporting those poor who had gained settlement in it by birth or residence for a certain period. An Act passed in 1662 provided that any newcomer in a parish could be ejected within forty days after his arrival unless he gave satisfactory evidence that he would not fall upon the parish for relief. Down to 1795 a laborer could move to a new village only if his own had given him a certificate acknowledging its responsibility for his support or if the other village had invited him. The control of the parish officers over his movements was only partly decreased by the Act of 1795, which provided that no one was to be removable until he had become chargeable to the parish, for any temporary distress still could bring about his ejection. Cf. Nicholls, *op. cit.,* I, 293-302; II, 118-22; *The Village Labourer,* pp. 88-96, 128-30.

[29] Nicholls, *op. cit.,* II, 137-39; Eden, *op. cit.,* pp. 121-25; *The Village Labourer,* pp. 137-43; Élie Halévy, *A History of the English People in 1815* (New York: Harcourt Brace and Co., 1924), p. 218; G. M. Trevelyan, *British History in the Nineteenth Century, 1782-1901* (London: Longmans, Green, and Co., 1934), pp. 148-50.

for the poverty resulting from the pressure of population upon subsistence. Poor relief, which gives the poor a degree of assurance that their offspring will not starve, only aggravates the distress; for allowances to the poor only re-distribute the available food without making any more food available, so that relatively, as population increases, subsistence is decreased.[30] As a palliative, but only as such, Malthus urges "the total abolition of all the present parish laws."[31] For "cases of extreme distress" there might be workhouses where assistance could be exchanged for labor,[32] but to discourage propagation, the rewards of indigence should not be made attractive. "Hard as it may appear, dependent poverty ought to be held disgraceful."[33] As a preliminary step toward withdrawing support from the poor, the government should decree "that no child born from any marriage, taking place after the expiration of a year from the date of the law; and no illegitimate child born two years from the same date, should ever be entitled to parish assistance."[34] Before "solemnization of a marriage," Malthus further suggests, the clergyman should warn the bride and groom of "the strong obligation on every man to support his own children. . . ."[35]

Malthus was not, however, rebuking the poor. He realized that they, and not the rich, were the victims of the Poor Laws. The poor "do submit to these regulations," but the upper classes do not and cannot fulfill their part of the contract: the poor sacrifice their liberty and receive no adequate return.[36] The abolition of the Poor Laws "would at any rate give liberty of action to the peasantry of England, which they can hardly be said to possess at present."[37]

The doctrines of political economy, among which the principle of population was to take a prominent place, had already designated poverty as the result of certain natural laws, the operation of which had best not be interfered with.

---

[30] *First Essay,* pp. 83-84.
[31] *Ibid.,* pp. 95-96.
[32] *Ibid.,* p. 97.
[33] *Ibid.,* p. 85.
[34] *Essay* (2d ed.), Bk. IV, chap. vii, p. 538.
[35] *Ibid.*
[36] *First Essay,* p. 99.
[37] *Ibid.,* p. 95.

The provision of free education for the poor was considered within the province of government,[38] but economists deprecated charity from the state or any governmental interference with prices or wages. Any attempt to fix a higher wage, it was asserted, would only diminish the demand for labor or so increase prices that there would be no advance in real wages.[39] Bentham, attacking Pitt's Poor Bill in 1797, had discouraged allowances to the poor as interfering with the benefits of free competition—as "putting the *idle* and *negligent* exactly upon a footing in point of prosperity and reward with the *diligent* and *industrious*" and consequently increasing "the multitude of the idle"[40]—and Burke would have barred those who could not compete in the labor market from any claim to support "according to the rules of commerce and the principles of justice," granting only that they might become objects of private charity.[41] The sacredness of the "natural" wage determined by supply and demand led Pitt to drop his Poor Bill and successfully oppose Whitbread's minimum wage.

It went [he said] to introduce legislative interference into that which ought to be allowed invariably to take its natural course. The greater freedom there was allowed in every kind of mercantile transactions, the more for the benefit of all parties.[42]

Malthus gave still more reason to believe that the Poor Laws were condemned by "the fixed laws of our nature" as futile or even dangerous. The *Essay* asserts that those "born after the division of property" must depend, for subsistence, on the "fund appropriated for the maintenance of labor," which is "the aggregate quantity of food possessed by the owners of the land beyond their own consumption," and that, in order to proportion as favorably as possible the number of non-landowners to the food available for their support, the subsistence granted each laborer and his family should be in

---

[38] *The Wealth of Nations*, II, 267-72.
[39] *Ibid.*, I, 142-44; Edmund Burke, *Thoughts and Details on Scarcity*, *The Works of Edmund Burke* (Boston: Little, Brown, and Co., 1866), V, 137-41, 156-57, and *passim;* Jeremy Bentham, *Observations on the Poor Bill* (London: William Clowes and Sons, 1838), pp. 6-7.
[40] *Ibid.*, pp. 7-8.
[41] Burke, *op. cit.*, pp. 145-46.
[42] Hansard, *Parliamentary History*, XXXIV (1800), 1428.

proportion to and entirely dependent upon his own labor.[43] Since any attempt to increase the laborer's share of food by means of public or private charity only encourages population and discourages industry, the number of laborers relative to the supply of food becomes even less favorable; whereas if wages were allowed to reach their "natural" level, that is, to be determined only by the ratio of numbers to the food exchangeable for their labor, moral restraint and industry would be enforced. Malthus, like Godwin, uses the word "natural" not only to indicate what is usual or even invariable but also in opposition to what is artificial or arbitrary. But for Malthus, since man is compelled by the instinct of self-preservation to establish marriage and property, these institutions, although man-made, are "natural" in that they are expedient; but just as Godwin sees no need for marriage and property and therefore calls them "arbitrary" or "positive," Malthus designates the Poor Laws as "positive" institutions.[44]

The harmony of Malthus's doctrine with the current objections to the "artificial" regulation of wages is further suggested by the *Edinburgh Review's* criticism of John Weyland's first attack on the *Essay: A Short Inquiry into the Policy, Humanity, and Past Effects of the Poor Laws* (1807). The burden of the review is that Weyland would "add to that mass of paltry devices and artificial regulations by which the great arrangements of society are already too much obstructed," that "all his schemes of reformation consist entirely of artificial regulations and restraints," whereas "the great point in all those arrangements ought to be, to free society as much as possible from burdensome restraints."[45] Weyland defends supplementing wages out of the rates so that, population being thus encouraged, there will always be a plentiful supply of cheap labor. Being able to secure labor at a low rate, he argues, the farmers will make greater profits and invest more capital, thus increasing production.[46] The reviewer replies that "the

---

43 *First Essay*, pp. 194-207; *Essay* (2d ed.), Bk. III, chap. ii, p. 379.
44 *First Essay*, pp. 89, 93, 199, and *passim*. Cf. *Political Justice* (1st ed.), I, 121; II, 600, 802, 878, and *passim*.
45 "Inquiry into the State of the Poor," *op. cit.*, pp. 101-02, 112.
46 [John Weyland], *A Short Inquiry into the Policy, Humanity and Past Effects of the Poor Laws* . . . (London: J. Hatchard and F. C. and J. Rivington and J. Asperne, 1807), pp. 10, 37-40, and *passim*. Weyland acknowledges his

condition of the laborer depends" not on the "absolute supply of food, but on its relative supply" and that "this supply will be great or small, according to the degree in which the preventive check to population prevails." The reviewer approves, therefore, of Malthus's plan for discontinuing the poor rates and suggests also that, upon six months' warning, every able-bodied laborer be "wholly excluded from parochial relief."[47]

It seems probable that even from the first the growing cost of poor relief[48] and its apparent futility in checking distress enforced the acceptance of Malthus's doctrine, although there is evidence that until after 1815 the landowners and tithe-owners were willing to put up with high poor rates for the sake of keeping the poor tractable and collecting high rents.[49] The critics, at least, pretty well agree that the rich welcomed release from moral as well as financial responsibility. "No wonder," exclaimed Southey, "that Mr. Malthus should be a fashionable philosopher!" He "calls for no sacrifice from the rich; on the contrary, he proposes to relieve them from their parish rates."[50] Malthus's doctrine, according to Hazlitt, "is certainly a very convenient [one for the rich]; and it is not to be wondered at, that it should have become so fashionable as it has." The miser "Sir W. Pulteney," Hazlitt adds in a footnote, "was firmly persuaded that the author of the Essay on Population was the greatest man that ever lived, and really wished to have bestowed some personal remuneration on Mr. M. as his political confessor, for having absolved him from all doubts and scruples in the exercise of his favorite virtue."[51] Godwin wondered no more than either Southey or Hazlitt at the reception of the *Essay.* "No wonder that [Mr. Malthus's] book is always to be found in the country seats of the court of aldermen, and in the palaces of the great." There never was

---

authorship in his *Observations on Mr. Whitbread's Poor Bill* . . . (London: J. Hatchard, F. C. and J. Rivington, and J. Asperne, 1807), title page and pp. 1-2.

47 "Inquiry into the State of the Poor," *op. cit.,* pp. 108-115.

48 The yearly cost of maintaining the poor rose from £1,250,000 in 1760 to £4,077,000 in 1802-1803. (*Report of the Royal Commission on Poor Laws and Relief of Distress* [London: His Majesty's Stationery Office, 1909], I, 83-84. Cf. Nicholls, *op. cit.,* II, 58, 139, 177.)

49 *The Village Labourer,* pp. 146, 155-58.

50 "Malthus's Essay on Population," *op. cit.,* pp. 300-01. Cf. Southey, "Inquiry into the Poor Laws," *op. cit.,* pp. 321-22.

51 *Reply,* p. 182. Cf. "Mr. Malthus," *op. cit.,* p. 298.

"so comfortable a preacher. . . ."[52] On the other hand, although Whitbread's Poor Bill of 1807 contained a provision for plural voting in vestry that would have given the wealthier members of the parish more power in determining the rates, and although in arguing for his bill Whitbread stressed the increasing cost of parochial relief,[53] the bill got only as far as committee; whereas a similar but less humane proposal won the support of the landlords in 1818.

CONDITIONS AFTER 1815

In the years following the end of the war, hard times again forced the ruling class to deal with the problem of poverty. Even before 1815 the majority of the workers had received only a meagre return for their labor, the profits of war time having gone to create fortunes for landlords and a new scale of living for the farmers.[54] With the spread of the Speenhamland system, the wages of the rural worker had been kept only at the maintenance level.

The ordinary village did not contain a mass of decently paid labourers and a surplus of labourers, from time to time redundant, for whom the parish had to provide as best it could. It contained a mass of labourers, all of them underpaid, whom the parish had to keep alive in the way most convenient to the farmers.[55]

The laborers in industry fared no better. In some industries the new machines were displacing skilled craftsmen with cheaper labor—often with women and children—and a growing number of workers were herded together in large factories, where adults and children alike toiled for twelve, fifteen, or even eighteen hours a day.[56] With the progress of the war,

---

52 William Godwin, *Of Population. An Enquiry Concerning the Power of Increase in the Numbers of Mankind* (London: Longman, Hurst, Rees, Orme, and Brown, 1820), p. 565. Cf. Charles Hall, *The Effects of Civilization* . . . (London: T. Ostell, 1805), pp. 313-14; Grahame, *op. cit.*, p. 34; Ensor, *op. cit.*, p. 85; P. B. Shelley, "Remarks on Mandeville," *Shelley's Literary and Philosophical Criticism*, ed. John Shawcross (London: Humphrey Milford, 1932), p. 2.
53 [Samuel] Whitbread, *Substance of a Speech on the Poor Laws* . . . (London: J. Ridgway, 1807), pp. 6, 54-57.
54 William Smart, *Economic Annals of the Nineteenth Century* (London: Macmillan and Co., 1910), I, 455; *The Village Labourer*, pp. 142-43.
55 *Ibid.*, p. 150.
56 G. D. H. Cole, *The Life of William Cobbett* (London: W. Collins Sons and

despite the profits of the industrialists, the manufacturing population experienced continual distress.[57] Taxes multiplied the expense of living. Carrying on the war by attacks on trade brought continual disorganization of industry, and the workers were the principal victims.[58] After the war the distress among the laborers grew even more acute. In both agriculture and manufacturing, production had outrun demand: the government no longer required food and manufactured material for the army, and the foreign market collapsed as well.[59] As usual in these situations, manufacturers shut down or went on short time, but only succeeded in further limiting their market.[60] Corn prices fell until the scanty harvest of 1816 sent them up again; but making little profit, because of the smallness of the yield, the farmers cut wages and set about reducing the allowances of the Speenhamland system.[61] Since rents had fallen more slowly than prices, many farmers were forced into bankruptcy and their workers left without employment.[62] Thousands of discharged soldiers crowded the labor market.[63] The Corn Laws, intended to perpetuate war prices, caused increases in price with which wages could not keep pace.[64] Taxes and consequently their indirect burden on the laborer increased to new proportions, and the depreciation of currency and fluctuation in the price of gold forced wages still closer to the starvation level.[65]

Again, as in 1795 and 1800, the ruling class took measures to suppress acts of violence and doctrines thought subversive

---

Co., 1927), pp. 195-97; Smart, *op. cit.,* I, 442-43, 493, 596-98; Halévy, *op. cit.,* pp. 229, 245-46; *The Town Labourer,* pp. 15-36, 144-47, and *passim.*

[57] Smart, *op. cit.,* I, 263-65, 271-76, and *passim.*

[58] *The Town Labourer,* p. 103.

[59] Smart, *op. cit.,* I, 494, 515, 529.

[60] *Ibid.,* pp. 491-92. Cf. Cole, *op. cit.,* p. 196.

[61] *The Village Labourer,* p. 160. Cf. *Weekly Political Register,* XXXI (October 5, 1816), 320-25; Smart, *op. cit.,* I, 489-90; Cole, *Life of William Cobbett,* p. 196; Halévy, *op. cit.,* p. 218.

[62] Smart, *op. cit.,* I, 455-56, 512-14; Cole, *Life of William Cobbett,* p. 196; *The Village Labourer,* p. 151.

[63] Smart, *op. cit.,* I, 539.

[64] *The Town Labourer,* pp. 108-09. Cf. Smart, *op. cit.,* I, 413, and J. S. Nicholson, *The History of the English Corn Laws* (London: Swan Sonnenschein and Co., 1904), pp. 52-53.

[65] Cole, *Life of William Cobbett,* pp. 196-97. Cf. *Weekly Political Register,* XXXI (August 3, 1816), 105-06; *The Town Labourer,* pp. 106-07; Smart, *op. cit.,* I, 530-31 and *passim.*

to the established system of property. Rioting broke out when, in 1816, scarcity forced up the price of wheat without giving the agricultural worker more employment or higher wages. The rioters assembled at night, and set fire to houses, barns, and ricks.[66] According to the London *Times* of May 25, "wages had been reduced to a rate lower than the magistrates thought reasonable, for the magistrates, after suppressing a riot near Downham, acquiesced in the propriety of raising wages, and released the offenders who had been arrested with a suitable remonstrance."[67] But as the violence of the riots increased, the work of suppression was carried on with increasing harshness. Beginning with the spring of 1817, "the newspapers . . . became full of accounts of 'risings,' riots, burnings of property, and shootings of labourers, not in one part of the country, but everywhere."[68] Of the prisoners taken after a battle in Littlefields, the Cambridge *Chronicle* for June 28 reports that "five were hung, five were transported for life, one was transported for fourteen years, three for seven years, and ten were imprisoned for twelve months in Ely gaol."[69] The Habeas Corpus was suspended in 1817, and three other coercion acts were passed in the same year.[70]

An ideology antagonistic to landed property can hardly be said to have motivated many of the rioters. It was simply that starvation drove them to violence.[71] But the followers of Thomas Spence drew special attention from the government for demanding "the expropriation of the landlords, the restoration of collective ownership of the land, and the establishment in each parish of a system of common cultivation."[72] In December, 1816, a riot which followed a meeting of the Spenceans was put down with force. Although the riot was a small affair, "the papers became full of sensational stories

---

66 *The Annual Register*, 1816, Chronicle, pp. 61-62, 66-68, 69-74, and *passim*; Smart, *op. cit.*, I, 489.
67 Cited in *The Village Labourer*, pp. 153-54.
68 Cole, *Life of William Cobbett*, p. 201. Cf. *Weekly Political Register*, American edition, XXX (May 18, 1816), 628-40; Smart, *op. cit.*, I, 548-54 and *passim; The Town Labourer*, pp. 87-94; Halévy, *op. cit.*, pp. 218-19.
69 Cited in *The Village Labourer*, p. 154.
70 Smart, *op. cit.*, I, 550-51.
71 The rioters' flag in Suffolk was inscribed "Bread or Blood." (*The Annual Register*, 1816, Chronicle, p. 67.)
72 Halévy, *op. cit.*, p. 219.

of a revolutionary plot"; the leaders were put on trial for high treason but acquitted for lack of evidence.[73] Probably the "revolutionary" doctrine that came closest to assuming any practical shape is that of Robert Owen, who blamed the failure of the market on inadequate wages[74] and attacked the "principle of individual gain" for limiting the amount of food made available to the workers;[75] but the landowners' antagonism toward any plan seeming to threaten their property rights worked against his proposed "Villages of Co-operation." These villages were to be "limited communities of individuals" created "on the principles of united labour and expenditure, [and] having their basis in agriculture. . . ."[76] Since the laborers would raise food and manufacture goods primarily for their own use, and sell only surplus products in the open market, their supply of food would no longer be limited by the speculation of capitalists.[77] Owen's plan had the support of powerful friends, who held that the villages could be realized without endangering the established system of property. The committee headed by the Duke of Kent and "selected from among the most respectable and intelligent public characters of all parties" depreciated the objection "that Mr. Owen's plans necessarilv involve a community of goods." Although Mr. Owen, the report of the committee continues, "has expressed on a former occasion some opinion in favour of a state of society in which a community of goods should exist, . . . he had never considered it as essential to the success of such an establishment as is now proposed. . . ." In any case "the present laws of real property make a community of profits from land quite impossible, and . . . the legislature are not likely to alter the laws in this respect upon any suggestion of Mr. Owen's."[78] But, as Owen increasingly

[73] Cole, *Life of William Cobbett*, pp. 212-13. Cf. *Weekly Political Register*, XXXI (December 14, 1816), 625-43; Smart, *op. cit.*, I, 551-52.

[74] Robert Owen, "Report to the County of Lanark" (1820), *The New Existence of Man Upon Earth. . . .* Part III (London: Effingham Wilson, 1854), Appendix, pp. vi-vii.

[75] Robert Owen, "Letter Published in the London Newspapers of July 30th, 1817," *A Supplementary Appendix to the First Volume of the Life of Robert Owen. . . .* (London: Effingham Wilson, 1858), I, 74-75.

[76] *Ibid.*, p. 69.

[77] Robert Owen, "Letter Published in the London Newspapers of August 9th, 1817," *A Supplementary Appendix*, p. 91.

[78] "Address of the Committee," London, August 23, 1819, *A Supplementary*

stressed the need of changing the system of property and wages,[79] the opposition implied in the report of the committee grew stronger, and the villages were never established.[80]

The feeling against social change, aroused especially by the forces that seemed to threaten property rights, apparently won Malthus new support. The *Quarterly Review* had opposed Malthus until, in 1817, it admitted itself won over by concessions Malthus had made and by new census figures showing that "in every county where the resources are in any way limited" the preventive and the positive checks had varied inversely;[81] but as early as 1813 it had realized that the *Essay* and the interests of the upper classes were in accord, for although depreciating Malthus's fear of the "phantom of population," it praised him "for the boldness with which he ha[d] opposed some errors of modern philanthropists, and for the just and popular arguments by which he ha[d] demonstrated the impossibility of supplying, from the contribution of the rich and idle, those means of subsistence which can only be secured by the labour of the industrious."[82] Then in 1816, after Sumner had praised Malthus's principle of population as God's method of ensuring the inequality that develops man's faculties in this world as preparation for the next,[83] the *Quarterly*—although still rejecting that principle as providing insufficient reward in this world—agreed with Sumner that inequality is the condition best suited to social progress.[84] And when the new statistics had finally effected the *Quarterly's* complete conversion, the reviewer welcomed the principle of population as providing "a general rule of reference" for dealing with all such matters as the poor law, and, thinking perhaps of Owen's proposals and the Spencean "plot," concluded that

---

Appendix, pp. 245-46. Cf., for the support of Owen's plan in principle, Sir Egerton Brydges, *The Population and Riches of Nations* ... (Paris: J. J. Paschoud, and London: Rob. Triphook, 1819), pp. 79-84.

[79] Cf. "Report to the County of Lanark," *op. cit.*

[80] Cole, *Life of Robert Owen,* pp. 20-30.

[81] "Malthus on Population," *Quarterly Review,* XVII (July, 1817), 372-73.

[82] "Comber on National Subsistence," *Quarterly Review,* X (October, 1813), 159.

[83] John Bird Sumner, *A Treatise on the Records of the Creation, and on the Moral Attributes of the Creator* ... (3d ed.; London: J. Hatchard and Son, 1825), II, 113-202.

[84] "Sumner's Prize Essay," *Quarterly Review,* XVI (October, 1816), 54.

it is no slight advantage to be provided with an incontrovertible answer
to all sweeping reformers; and to know on positive grounds that the
face of civilized society must always remain uniform in its principle
lineaments, and be distinguished by the same features which it has hitherto borne; that our business therefore is to lessen or remove its blemishes,
and to prevent their growing into deformities; but that we can no more
organize a community without poverty, and its consequence, severe
labour, than we can organize a body without natural infirmities, or add a
limb to the human frame.[85]

In view of the war England had just endured and the widespread hunger and hunger-riots, it is difficult to share the reviewer's enthusiasm for "the face of civilized society," but
Malthus had acclaimed self-interest as the ruling social
principle.

In the years following 1815, it seems, just as at the turn
of the century, the fear of change enforced Malthus's justification of the system of private property; but after the war
the Poor Laws were less highly regarded as a means of preserving property rights. The inadequacy of the Speenhamland
system to solve the problem of poverty is evidenced not only
by the rioting among the laborers but by the efforts of the
upper classes to curtail relief.

Both the number of paupers [the Committee of the House of Commons on the Poor Laws reported in 1817] and the amount of money
levied by assessment were progressively increasing, while the situation of
the poor did not seem to have been in a corresponding degree improved;
and they were of the opinion that, while the existing poor laws and the
system under which they were administered remained unchanged, there
did not exist any power of arresting the progress of this increase till it
should no longer be found possible to augment the sums raised by assessment.[86]

The law of settlement was strictly enforced,[87] and in 1818 an
act was passed to give the wealthy more power in administer-
ing the rates. Although Whitbread's Poor Bill of 1807 would
have given additional voting power in vestry to those paying
higher assessments, it was not voted on; but in 1818 plural

---

85 "Malthus on Population," *op. cit.,* pp. 401-02.
86 Smart, *op. cit.,* I, 579.
87 *The Village Labourer,* pp. 154-55.

voting in vestry was finally established,[88] and in 1819 "select vestries" were authorized to control relief, with salaried overseers to administer it.[89] In 1818 and 1819, apparently, as suggested by the fate of other Poor-Law legislation proposed to the Committee or even introduced into Parliament,[90] the interest of the ruling class with regard to the Poor Laws was largely in curtailing expenditure.

The influence of Malthus favored the withdrawal of relief and opposed other methods of solving the problem of poverty; and it seems probable that the fear of overpopulation was at least partly responsible for the adoption of the Acts of 1818 and 1819 and the rejection of other measures. Until the end of the eighteenth century a large and increasing population was generally regarded as desirable and necessary for the prosperity and defense of the country; and until the first census in 1801 there was even a fear that the population was decreasing, the Poor Laws being thought of, more often than not, as checking rather than encouraging population— especially because they interfered with the mobility of labor.[91] Malthus's first attack on the Poor Laws as making for overpopulation was re-enforced by the official figures in 1801, but until after 1815, war-time prosperity apparently deterred the ruling classes from pressing the charge that the Poor Laws had created a redundant population. In 1816 and 1817, however, Robert Owen reports, "there was an outcry and great alarm created by the Malthusians, who asserted that . . . the sufferings of the poor and the want of employment . . . arose from an excess of population."[92] The *Quarterly,* we have seen, welcomed Malthus's principle as providing "a general rule of reference" for dealing with all such matters as the Poor Laws.

The importance of having such a rule established may be best appreciated by reflecting on the consequences of wanting, or neglecting

---

[88] Nicholls, *op. cit.,* II, 192-93; Smart, *op. cit.,* I, 639.

[89] Nicholls, *op. cit.,* II, 193-200. For the effects of this Act, see *The Village Labourer,* pp. 158-59.

[90] Smart, *op. cit.,* I, 638-40, 705-07.

[91] G. Talbot Griffith, *Population Problems in the Age of Malthus* (Cambridge [England]: The University Press, 1926), pp. 129-41.

[92] *The Life of Robert Owen by Himself,* p. 201. Cf. pp. 266, 280.

it. These were predicted by Mr. Malthus at a period when there was an extraordinary demand for men, and very little disposition to suppose the possibility of any evil arising out of the redundancy of population. But his remarks on the nature and effects of the poor laws have been in the most striking manner confirmed by the experience of the years 1815, 1816, and 1817.[93]

The Committee of the House of Commons on the Poor Laws, which refused Owen a hearing for his Villages of Co-operation, seems to have been dominated by Malthusian thought. "The majority of the members," according to Owen, "had made up their minds, influenced by the Malthusian irrational notions of over-population, to depress the poor out of existence, instead of finding them employment at decent wages."[94] Sir Egerton Brydges, a member of the Committee, testifies that among the objections "(felt, rather than clearly expressed,) to the employment of the Poor on waste lands, was the fear to hasten overstepping [of the limits of production]"[95]—a notion irrational enough but frequently inferred from the *Essay*. And in 1816 Lord Brougham, another member of the Committee, had argued against outdoor relief by pointing out that it "removes the check upon improvident marriages, and tends to multiply the number of people beyond the means of subsistence."[96]

Objections to Malthus's *ESSAY*

The number of replies testifies that not all of Malthus's readers were ready to blame poverty on "nature" and leave its amelioration to the poor themselves. Even critics who were no more sympathetic with Godwin's doctrine than Malthus, refused to believe that the scope for "improvement" should be as limited by nature as the *Essay* maintained and were shocked by the "inhumanity" of Malthus's proposal to withdraw relief from the poor. Thus, although the means suggested for enabling the poor to obtain more food may vary, there is almost unanimous agreement among the earlier critics

[93] "Malthus on Population," *op. cit.*, p. 401.
[94] *The Life of Robert Owen by Himself*, p. 215.
[95] *Op. cit.*, pp. 81-82.
[96] Hansard, *Parliamentary Debates*, XXXIII (1816), 1115.

that institutions bear more responsibility for poverty than Malthus would allow and that the Poor Laws must be kept, at least until some plan for improvement has been realized. In general, although the distinction cannot be made consistently, the criticism of institutions may be considered a reply to Malthus's first edition and the defense of the Poor Laws a reply to his second.

These two lines of argument characterize the replies of 1798-1821. The institutions attacked, however, range from private property to taxes that limit the profit of the farmer. Godwin blames poverty on the political and economic power of the ruling classes;[97] and, arguing for increased production of food as well as more equitable distribution, Hall,[98] Hazlitt, Shelley,[99] Owen,[100] and Ensor[101] also point out the unjust effects of private property or of the power currently attached to its possession. But other critics, who defend the power of the propertied classes, blame the shortage of food not so much on the system of ownership and distribution as on the institutions that limit production. Young,[102] Gardner,[103] Anderson,[104] and Weyland,[105] all of whom defend the interests of the proprietor, criticize restrictions that, by threatening his profits, give the farmer less incentive to invest his time and money in producing more food. Although less concerned than these writers with the interests of any particular group, Southey,[106]

[97] *Thoughts Occasioned by the Perusal of Dr. Parr's Spital Sermon* . . . (London: G. G. and J. Robinson, 1801) ; *Of Population.*

[98] *Op. cit.;* Charles Hall, *The Effects of Civilization on the People in European States, with an Appendix Containing Observations on the Principal Conclusion in Mr. Malthus's Essay on Population* (2d ed.; London: M. Jones and Craddock and Co., 1813).

[99] *A Philosophical View of Reform, Works,* VII, 32-33, 41, 50-54; *Proposals for an Association, Works,* V, 226 and *passim.*

[100] Robert Owen, *A New View of Society* . . . (3d ed.; London: Longman, Hurst, Rees, Orme, and Brown, 1817) ; "Report to the County of Lanark," *op. cit.;* "Letter Published . . . July 30th, 1817," *op. cit.;* "Letter Published . . . August 9th, 1817," *op. cit.*

[101] *Op. cit.*

[102] *The Question of Scarcity; An Inquiry into the Propriety of Applying Wastes to the Better Maintenance and Support of the Poor.*

[103] *Op. cit.*

[104] James Anderson, *A Calm Investigation of the Circumstances That Have Led to the Present Scarcity* . . . (2d ed.; London: John Cumming, 1801).

[105] *A Short Inquiry;* John Weyland, *The Principles of Population and Production* . . . (London: Baldwin, Cradock, and Jay, 1816).

[106] "Malthus's Essay on Population," *op. cit.;* "Inquiry into the Poor Laws," *op. cit.*

Jarrold,[107] Ingram,[108] Gray,[109] Grahame,[110] and Brydges[111] do not challenge the right of the ruling class to limit the amount of food made available to the poor and, as a remedy for overpopulation, rely largely on the more complete utilization of resources at home and abroad or, what amounts to a means to this end, emigration. With regard to the criticism of institutions, therefore, the critics of 1798-1821 are more likely to agree not on the *means* of improvement—that is, upon the institutions obstructing the removal of "vice and misery"—but that the *degree* of improvement that is possible, or "natural," is much greater than Malthus would admit. Like Gray, they wish to "dispell th[e] gloom from every mind. . . ."[112] However various their proposed reforms, radical and conservative critics alike maintain that the world is a better place than Malthus would have them believe: that God or nature does not demand the continued suffering and immorality of a large portion of humanity.

Although horror at what seemed to be the heartlessness of Malthus's Poor-Law proposal also unifies most of the critics of 1798-1821, their arguments for poor relief show the same predilections as their attacks on institutions. Both radical and conservative critics, for instance, defend the Poor Laws as (1) restoring to the poor at least part of the rightful share of food denied them by the system of employment and wages

---

107 T. Jarrold, *Dissertations on Man* . . . (London: Cadell and Davis, and Burditt, 1806).

108 Robert Acklom Ingram, *Disquisitions on Population* . . . (London: J. Hatchard, 1808).

109 S[imon] Gray, *The Happiness of States* . . . ([2d ed.]; London: J. Hatchard and Son, and Longman and Co.; Edinburgh: A. Constable and Co., and Waugh and Innes, 1819), p. 357; George Purves [pseud. for Simon Gray], *Gray versus Malthus* . . . (London: Longman, Hurst, Rees, Orme, and Brown; Edinburgh: Archibald Constable and Co., 1818). According to his own testimony in the prefaces of both *Gray versus Malthus* and *The Happiness of States,* Gray wrote the latter in 1804. It was first published in 1815, and supplies most of the material for *Gray versus Malthus.*

110 *Op. cit.*

111 *Op. cit.*

112 *Gray versus Malthus,* p. 390. There are frequent comments on the pessimism occasioned by the *Essay.* Cf. Ingram, *op. cit.,* pp. 131-32; Ensor, *op. cit.,* pp. 135-36, 177, 258-59; Godwin, *Thoughts,* p. 54; Godwin, *Of Population,* p. 27. "A gentleman," Gray relates, "who was completely overrun with hypochondria, told me, when the Essay on Population was republished, with the tour of human misery added to it, that it had given him such pleasure, he had read it over three times, and meant to read it again." (*Gray versus Malthus,* p. 353.)

and (2) as decreasing the danger of uprisings among the laboring class. But whereas the first group defends relief[113] largely as a means of granting the right to subsistence denied the laborer by an unjust and therefore undesirable system of wages, the second group, while often admitting that this system curtails the worker's right to subsistence, defends it as expedient—especially for the increased production of food— and supports the Poor Laws as at once remedying the defects of the system and, by keeping the poor contented, securing it against change. On the other hand the writers of the first group deprecate violence, and approve of the Poor Laws as preventing it, because they wish a *change* in the system of property or employment. Shelley, for instance, agreeing with Godwin that reason—or an accurate calculation of consequences—and the resulting disinterestedness are necessary to improvement, opposes violent revolution as blurring foresight with passion.[114]

---

113 Owen is an exception. Although defending the poor's right to subsistence, he attacks the Poor Laws as obscuring a calculation of consequences, and proposes, in their place, the employment of the poor, when necessary, on public works. (*A New View of Society,* pp. 141 ff.)

114 *A Philosophical View of Reform,* pp. 50-54. Cf. *Political Justice* (1st ed.), I, 103; II, 878-93 and *passim.*

CHAPTER III

HAZLITT'S LETTERS ON THE POOR LAWS

In the "Advertisement" prefacing the *Reply,* Hazlitt grants "the diffuseness, the repetitions, and want of method to be found in these letters . . . [and] the great length to which they have run";[1] but although the parts sometimes overlap in citing both the same evidence and the same conclusions, Hazlitt's arrangement of his material is a useful one to follow in studying his views on population and their background. The first three letters introduce the principal ideas developed more fully in the later parts, but are especially helpful in distinguishing Hazlitt's conception of human motives from Godwin's and Malthus's and in illustrating Hazlitt's method of argument. In the fourth and fifth letters and in the "Extracts" Hazlitt's division of his subject corresponds to that made by other critics and facilitates comparison with them.

In the first letter, which was provoked by Whitbread's "proposed alterations in the system of Poor Laws,"[2] Hazlitt not only attacks these proposals but adds that, since they have been put forward "under the auspices of [Mr. Malthus's] discoveries," he will reveal the *Essay* as "the most complete specimen of *illogical,* crude and contradictory reasoning, that perhaps was ever offered to the notice of the public."[3] In the second letter, rather than getting on with this process, Hazlitt writes "On the Originality of Mr. Malthus's Essay" in an effort to discredit Malthus through the charge of plagiarism.[4] Hazlitt devotes the third letter to ridiculing Malthus's argument against "schemes of Utopian improvement."[5] The fourth letter, "On the General Tendency of Population to Excess," centers on the problem of Malthus's ratios,[6] and the

---

1 *Reply,* p. 179.
2 *Ibid.,* p. 181.
3 *Ibid.,* p. 186.
4 *Ibid.,* pp. 187-98. Cf. *Political Essays,* pp. 337-34, and "Mr. Malthus," *op. cit.,* pp. 107-08.
5 *Reply,* pp. 198-206. Cf. *Political Essays,* pp. 343-50, and "Mr. Malthus," *op. cit.,* pp. 105-07.
6 *Reply,* pp. 206-32. Cf. *Political Essays,* pp. 332-37, and "Mr. Malthus," *op. cit.,* pp. 109-11.

fifth, in which Hazlitt questions "Whether Vice and Misery
are the Necessary Consequences of, and the Only Checks to,
the Principle of Population," analyzes the factors affecting the
prudential check.[7] The "Extracts" and accompanying commentary offer further illustrations of "contradictions" and
"inconsistencies" already pointed out in the letters, but here
Hazlitt is concerned mainly with showing (1) the power of
the employer to keep wages at the subsistence level or lower
and (2) the consequent futility and injustice of discontinuing
poor relief in order to try to restore a "natural" wage.[8]

HAZLITT'S ATTACK ON WHITBREAD; HIS EXPLANATION OF HUMAN BEHAVIOR

Hazlitt devotes most of the first letter to attacking two of
Whitbread's proposals—(1) to give the largest contributors
more control of the poor fund and (2) to establish a national
system of education—but promises that, because of the selfishness Malthus has encouraged, the other letters will destroy his
arguments as inconsistent and absurd. Hazlitt objects less to
Whitbread's plan in itself than to the attitude toward the poor
which he thinks it represents. Whitbread's proposed savings
banks for the laborer, national system of education, and more
generous law of settlement do not suggest "cold, philosophical
indifference"[9] toward the poor; but Whitbread, persuaded by
Malthus, believes that the "earth does not produce where-
withal" to give "every peasant . . . a pullet in his kettle
. . . . Whatever [he adds] may be the first impulses of our
feeling, in order to do good, we must chastize and reduce them
within the sphere of action."[10] The poor, Hazlitt replies, "are
naturally despised" and their interests "at best but coldly and
remotely felt by the other classes of society," and the *Essay*
"has done all that was wanting to increase this indifference
and apathy . . . , [having] form[ed] selfishness into a regular code" supported by "metaphysical distinctions and cobwebs

---

7 *Reply*, pp. 232-84. Cf. "Mr. Malthus," *op. cit.*, pp. 108-09.
8 *Reply*, pp. 285-364. Cf. *Political Essays*, pp. 350-57, and "Mr. Malthus,"
op. cit., p. 111.
9 *Ibid.*, pp. 185-86.
10 *Op. cit.*, pp. 7-8.

of philosophy."[11] As long as the reasoned indifference taught by Malthus and affirmed by Whitbread "subsists in its full force, . . . any serious attempt at bettering the condition of the poor will be ineffectual" or even disastrous.[12] To give the largest contributors more control of the poor fund, as Whitbread suggested, would be a step back toward feudalism, and even the national system of education would be prevented from really helping the poor.

Hazlitt's objection to "cold, philosophic indifference" rests on premises that are basic in his political and economic doctrines. Since Hazlitt does not believe that men could be consistently motivated to serve the greatest happiness of the greatest number, he does not predict, with Godwin, a "perfect" society; but within the limits of possibility, the improvement of society, he believes, depends to a large degree on "philanthropy" or "benevolence" or "disinterestedness." "Naturally," Hazlitt writes in *An Essay on the Principles of Human Action* (1805), the human mind is "disinterested, or . . . interested in the welfare of others in the same way, and from the same direct motives by which [one is] impelled to pursuit of [his] own interest." Voluntary actions, unlike involuntary ones, do not arise solely from one's desire to avoid pain and to find pleasure, as Locke and his followers hold, but may be determined by the "idea" of good independent of any reference to one's own pleasure or pain. ". . . The mind is naturally interested in it's own welfare in a particular mechanical manner, only as far as related to it's past, or present impressions";[13] for, since the sensations a person will experience in the future cannot react mechanically upon his present self, only the imagination can connect the present self with the future self, and therefore it alone can produce ideas to motivate voluntary action. There being no mechanical sympathy with one's future sensations, "something in the very idea of good or evil [must] naturally excite . . . desire or aversion," and

---

[11] *Reply,* pp. 181-82.
[12] *Ibid.,* p. 182 and *passim.*
[13] *An Essay on the Principles of Human Action, Works,* I, 1. Cf. Horace Williston, "Hazlitt as a Critic of the 'Modern Philosophy,'" (Unpublished Ph. D. dissertation, Dept. of English, University of Chicago, 1938), pp. 205 ff.

there must be, consequently, the same psychological basis for interested and disinterested action.[14]

It was not, then, because he thought man necessarily selfish, that Hazlitt rejected Godwin's doctrine of universal benevolence but because reason seemed inadequate as a motivating force. Godwin, Hazlitt points out, "conceived too nobly of his fellows," placing "the human mind on an elevation, from which it commands a view of the whole line of moral consequences; and requir[ing] it to conform its acts to the larger and more enlightened conscience which it has thus acquired. He absolves man from the gross and narrow ties of sense, custom, authority, private and local attachment, in order that he may devote himself to the boundless pursuit of universal benevolence."[15] Since one pursues a good, either for himself or another, only from "having an idea of it sufficiently warm and vivid to excite in [him] an emotion of interest, or passion," man's disinterestedness must be limited well short of universality. Although a child first pursues his own good "not because it is his, but because it is *good* [,] . . . he prefers his own gratification to that of others . . . because he has a more distinct idea of his wants and pleasures than theirs" and consequently an emotion of interest and passion.[16] If one pursues "the good of others, of a relative, of a friend, of family, a community, or of mankind," it is because his idea of the good is accompanied by a similar emotion. Therefore, the universalizing of benevolence or disinterestedness on the basis of a calculation of consequences is impossible. Since reason can be only a guide to morality, since the moral life must derive its impulse from the affections, truly benevolent actions cannot be extended indefinitely.[17]

Although relinquishing the possibility of complete disinterestedness, Hazlitt does not, like Malthus, fall back upon faith in a *selfish* calculation of consequences as the "moving spirit" of society. There is, it is true, a certain similarity in Hazlitt's

---

14 *An Essay on the Principles of Human Action*, pp. 9-12. Cf. Williston, *op. cit.*, p. 211.
15 "William Godwin," *The Spirit of the Age, Works*, XI, 18-19.
16 *An Essay on the Principles of Human Action*, p. 12.
17 "Jeremy Bentham," *The Spirit of the Age, Works*, XI, 8-10.

and Malthus's depreciation of the power of a calculation of consequences to control the passions or affections. The strength of the sexual passion, Malthus asserts, is such that the good of society as a whole is too remote to enforce the preventive check when parents are sure of society's supporting their children; therefore a system of private property forcing every parent to support his own children becomes expedient.[18] Hazlitt, however, believes that even the prospect of not being able to support one's children will not enforce the preventive check unless "circumstances" of "comfort and decency" have fostered the "habit" of prudence[19]—and that these circumstances and this habit will not be realized as long as self-love, instead of benevolence, determines the treatment of the poor. In "bringing down the revolutionary philosophy," as Crane Brinton phrases it, "to the level of human nature,"[20] Hazlitt, therefore, is attacking the rationalism of both Godwin and Malthus but at the same time placing much the same evaluation as Godwin on benevolence as necessary to improvement.

The reason that Hazlitt objects to "forming selfishness into a regular code" is evident, for he believes (1) that man has secured his rights only "by the *wisdom* and *virtue* of the *enlightened* and *disinterested* part of mankind" combating the "pride, bigotry, and selfishness" of the others,[21] and (2) that the *disinterestedness* or *virtue* necessary to put *enlightenment* or *wisdom* to the service of society is a matter of "habitual cultivation." When Hazlitt writes "that the human mind is naturally benevolent," he does not mean that we are born with "good wishes for we know not whom," but simply that "there is a natural connection between the idea of happiness and the desire for it, independently of any particular attachment to the person who is to feel it." Only this disposition of the mind is inherent; the "actual desire of good" depends upon the acquired knowledge of what is good. "Independently of habit and association, the strength of the affection excited is in proportion to the strength of the idea, and does not at all depend on the person to whom it relates except indirectly and

---

18 *First Essay*, pp. 185 ff.
19 *Reply*, pp. 314 ff.
20 *Op. cit.*, p. 132.
21 "What Is the People?" *Political Essays, Works*, VII, 270. My italics.

by implication."[22] On the other hand, one may be motivated
not by an idea of particular good but by an idea abstracted
from "knowledge of various goods."[23] That is, one may trans-
fer "the feeling of real interest in a number of things conducive
to [a] person's welfare to the abstract idea of his good in
general."[24] Thus, "refined" or "artificial" self-love or "refined" benevolence implies that a person is striving for his own
or for others' happiness, not because the idea of his or their
good in itself excites his affections, but because with the idea of
his or their happiness he associates the feeling derived from
various "particular" or "real" goods. "In this case [such an
idea] will owe all it's power as a motive to habit, or association; for it is so immediately or in itself no longer than while
it implies a sentiment, or real feeling representative of good,
and only in proportion to the degree of force and depth which
this feeling has."[25] The extension of benevolence beyond the
"natural" preference for a particular good without reference
to the person to whom it relates, depends, therefore, upon "an
habitual cultivation of the natural disposition of the mind to
sympathize with the feelings of others by constantly taking an
interest in those which we know, and imagining others that we
do not know, [whereas] the other feeling of abstract self-
interest, that is in the degree in which it generally subsists,
must be caused by a long narrowing of the mind to our own
particular feelings and interests, and a voluntary insensibility
to everything which does not immediately concern our-
selves."[26]

HAZLITT'S ATTACK ON MALTHUS'S ORIGINALITY

Most of the second letter is written to diminish Malthus's
influence by tracing the acceptance of his doctrines to unworthy
motives or to impractical thinking and by showing that Malthus has said nothing on the subject of population but what is
obvious or what had been said before. The truth of Malthus's
doctrine, of course, is not to be weighed by the motives or

22 *An Essay on the Principles of Human Action*, p. 12.
23 *Ibid.*, p. 13.
24 *Ibid.*, p. 15.
25 *Ibid.*, p. 13.
26 *Ibid.*, pp. 14-15.

mentality of his followers, or by the extent to which it had been anticipated, but this method of detraction is both typical of Malthus's critics, although not of Malthus himself, and consistent with Hazlitt's explanation of human behavior. Evidently Hazlitt is using it to give the reader "an idea of [a good] sufficiently warm and vivid to excite in [him] an emotion of interest, or passion."[27] the immediate "good" being the reading of his *Reply* and the eventual one the rejection of Malthus's procedure for dealing with poverty. In the "Advertisement" prefacing the *Reply,* Hazlitt mentions that its style has been objected to as "too flowery, and full of attempts at description," and that "some of the observations may be thought too severe and personal," but he justifies the style and the severity of the attack as necessary to secure a hearing for his argument. He has "endeavoured to make [his] book as amusing as the costiveness of [his] genius would permit," for a "dry and formal" work will lack readers. Although "the abuse, of which there is to be sure a plentiful sprinkling, is not . . . unmerited or unsupported," he should have preferred to attack the work without attacking the author; but since the public will not trouble itself "about abstract reasonings, or calm, dispassionate inquiries after truth," he decided that "the thing was impossible."[28]

The *Essay,* therefore, figures in the *Reply* as "a work of . . . base tendency" disguising "the little, low, rankling malice of a parish-beadle, or the overseer of a workhouse . . . in the garb of philosophy" and replete with "false logic . . . buried under a heap of garbled calculations. . . ." That "such a miserable reptile performance should ever have crawled to that height of reputation which it has reached" can be explained, Hazlitt believes, only by selfishness, aversion to schemes of perfection, and impracticality among its readers. Like other critics Hazlitt sees the *Essay* as "a source of continual satisfaction" among "certain classes of society" whom it relieves "from [any] troublesome feelings" for the poor, and as gratifying to "a low and narrow jealousy, which makes [some minds] glad . . . to escape from the contemplation

---

[27] *An Essay on the Principles of Human Action,* p. 12.
[28] *Reply,* p. 179.

of magnificent scenes of visionary excellence, to hug themselves in their own indifference and apathy, and to return once more to their natural level." For the reception of the *Essay* "among thinking men," however, Hazlitt finds "it . . . not easy to account," except in so far as some minds "from a habit of extreme abstraction and over-refined speculation, unsupported by actual observation or a general knowledge of practical subjects, . . . [are] dazzled and confounded by any striking fact which thwarts [their] previous conclusions."[29]

The early critics frequently charge Malthus or his followers with this "impracticality" or failure to check their conclusions with observable phenomena, for it is observable that population and subsistence increase, not at widely divergent rates, but at approximately the same rate. As long, therefore, as Hazlitt insists that the ratios have no practical significance unless the arithmetical and geometrical rates of increase are actually and simultaneously achieved, he is in a much better position, than he would be otherwise, (1) to dismiss the principle of population as merely an axiomatic proposition without any application to such practical matters as improving the condition of the poor and (2) to press his charge of plagiarism.

Although the *Essay* has been hailed as a "discovery," Hazlitt asserts, Malthus's principle is simply a truism, and whatever remained obscure about it had been cleared up by Wallace. Hazlitt, like Coleridge and Southey before him, does "not see what there is to discover on the subject, after reading the genealogical table of Noah's descendants, and knowing that the world is round."[30] Coleridge, writing in the margin of Malthus's second edition,[31] protests that the meaning of the ratios could be expressed by "a proportion which no one in his senses would consider as other than axiomatic," and to express this proportion, "supposes a married couple to have six chil-

---

29 *Ibid.*, p. 188. Cf. "Mr. Malthus," *op. cit.*, pp. 106, 112.

30 *Reply*, p. 189. This is the only one of Hazlitt's arguments that Bonar mentions; in fact, he seems completely to identify Hazlitt's objection to the *Essay* with Coleridge's and Southey's. (Bonar, *op. cit.*, pp. 85, 372, 394.)

31 Coleridge's copy is in the British Museum, but most of his marginal notes are quoted in Bonar, *op. cit.*, pp. 371-74. See also George Reuben Potter, "Unpublished Marginalia in Coleridge's Copy of Malthus's *Essay on Population*," *PMLA*, LI, (1936), 1061-68; and Kenneth Curry, "A Note on Coleridge's Copy of Malthus," *PMLA*, LIV (1939), 613-15; and Place, *op. cit.*, Notes on Appendix A, pp. 294-96.

dren . . . and . . . all their posterity to marry and increase in the same proportion. . . ."[32] And Southey, for whose direction it seems probable that these marginalia were written,[33] repeats Coleridge's complaint that so much "verbiage" had been written to prove an "axiomatic proposition."[34] But Malthus admits, even in his first *Essay,* the obviousness of population pressure, and justifies the *Essay* as examining the forms this pressure may assume under different social and economic conditions.[35] What Coleridge and Southey overlook, and what Hazlitt refuses to credit Malthus with suggesting, is that, however obvious may be the discrepancy between the biologically possible rate of population increase and the food production possible for a limited territory, and however obvious it may be that subsistence and population actually increase not at different but at approximately equal rates, it was not obvious —at least to Coleridge and Southey and to other critics as well—how the ratios indicate (1) that the *pressure* of population is nevertheless *on subsistence*—or, according to the qualification made by Malthus himself, on the level of living, with subsistence as only the ultimate check—and (2) that, other factors remaining constant, population will increase or decrease as more or less food is made available.

Not granting this implication of the ratios, Hazlitt can more readily disparage the *Essay.* as a repetition of Robert Wallace's views on population as found in his *Various Prospects of Mankind, Nature, and Providence.*

The most important argument that I shall adduce [Malthus had granted in his first edition] is certainly not new. The principles on which it depends have been explained in part by Hume, and more at large by Dr. Adam Smith. It has been advanced and applied to the present subject, though not with its proper weight, or in the most forcible point of view, by Mr. Wallace: and it may probably have been stated by many writers that I have never met with. I should certainly therefore not

---

[32] On p. 8 of Coleridge's copy of the *Essays:* cf. Bonar, *op. cit.,* p. 372, and Potter, *op. cit.,* pp. 1062-63.

[33] As Curry points out (*op. cit.,* pp. 614-15), Coleridge's advice, "Quote this paragraph as the first sentence of your Review . . . ," and verbal resemblances between the marginalia and Southey's article suggest that Coleridge had been writing his comments for Southey's use.

[34] Southey, "Malthus's Essay on Population," *op. cit.,* p. 293. Cf. Hall, *The Effects of Civilization* (2d ed.), p. 343.

[35] *First Essay,* Preface, p. iii.

think of advancing it again, though I mean to place it in a point of view in some degree different from any that I have hitherto seen, if it had ever been fairly and satisfactorily answered.[36]

Although acknowledging this acknowledgment,[37] Hazlitt, intent on his *ad hominem* attack and misunderstanding (or mis-representing) Malthus's principle, presses his charge of plagiarism by quoting a long passage from the *Various Prospects*. Wallace, he points out, turns regretfully from any hope of realizing a "perfect form" of government.

Under a perfect government, the inconveniences of having a family would be so intirely removed, children would be so well taken care of, and every thing become so favourable to populousness, that though some sickly seasons or dreadful plagues in particular climates might cut off multitudes, yet in general, mankind would increase so prodigiously, that the earth would at last be overstocked, and become unable to support its numerous inhabitants.[38]

Until such a time, Wallace grants, this kind of government would turn the earth into "a paradise in the literal sense," transforming "the greatest part of it . . . into delightful and fruitful gardens";[39] but the memory of these happy times, when laws were perfectly obeyed and plenty existed for all, would make the inevitable "vice and confusion" only more distressing, as rebelling against "cruel and unnatural" regulations to check population, the people resorted at last to war, and "the deaths of such as f[e]ll in battle, le[ft] sufficient provisions for the survivors, and ma[d]e room for others to be born."[40]

This "melancholy situation," Wallace decides, would be more "unnatural" than the "present calamities" suffered by society. ". . . Our present distresses" may be called "natural," having resulted from man's abuse of his liberty and being providence's means of (1) punishing such vice and (2) preventing "the earth's being overstocked, and men being laid

---

[36] *First Essay*, p. 8. Cf. *Essay* (2d ed.), Preface, p. iii.
[37] *Reply*, p. 189, n.
[38] [Robert Wallace], *Various Prospects of Mankind, Nature, and Providence* (London: A. Millar, 1761), p .114. Quoted in *Reply*, p. 190.
[39] *Ibid.*, p. 117. Quoted in *Reply*, p. 191.
[40] *Ibid.*, pp. 119-20. Quoted in *Reply*, p. 192.

under the cruel necessity of killing one another"; whereas it "seems wholly unnatural," that is, not agreeable to the methods of "a favourable providence," that a paradisaical society living in "universal friendship and concord . . . should be overturned, not by the vices of men, or their abuse of liberty, but by the order of nature itself. . . ." Given such "primary determinations in nature" as "a limited earth, a limited degree of fertility and the continual increase of mankind," some adaptation of human affairs must be made to "these original constitutions." Of the alternatives of (1) letting the human race increase as it could under a perfect government and ending in overwhelming disaster or of (2) "permitting vice, or the abuse of liberty in the wisdom of providence, [to prevent mankind from multiplying] so greatly as to overstock the earth," the former is "more contrary to just proportion," that is, apparently, to Wallace's conception of a benevolent providence.[41] Therefore, "jealous and selfish politicians" have no need to fear the establishment of governments that will "disappoint them of their intention to sacrifice the interest of mankind to their own avarice or ambition," for "we need not doubt but providence will make use of [the vices of mankind], for preventing the establishment of governments which are by no means suitable to the present circumstances of the earth."[42]

Here, says Hazlitt, we have the "same argument" and the same application as found in the *Essay,* Malthus not even having drawn from the argument "an important inference of which [Wallace] was not at all aware.[43] This "same argument" that Hazlitt has in mind seems to be that, since food and population increase at different rates, vice and misery are constantly needed to keep population down to the level of subsistence, lest population get such a head start that only something cataclysmic in the way of positive checks could enable subsistence to catch up. The "imposing air of accuracy and profundity" carried by mathematical terms works on the imagination, so that men overlook the absurdity of such disproportionate rates of increase, and fearing that every increase in food made available to the laboring class will result in a much

---

41 *Ibid.,* pp. 120-22. Quoted in *Reply,* p. 193.
42 *Ibid.,* pp. 124-25. Quoted in *Reply,* p. 194.
43 *Reply,* p. 194.

greater increase in population, the ruling classes are loathe to relieve poverty.

[Mr. Malthus] has alarmed men's minds with confused apprehensions on the subject, by setting before their eyes, in an orderly series, the malignant nature and terrible effects of population, which are perpetually increasing as it goes on; and they are ready to assent to every scheme that promises to keep these dreadful evils at a distance from them.[44]

That such an actual and increasing discrepancy between food and numbers should exist is, according to Hazlitt, "all that is *practically* meant by a geometrical and arithmetical series," and although this series has been claimed for Mr. Malthus as his own, Wallace completely anticipated him in this respect by saying "that let one ratio increase as fast as it would, the other would increase much faster. . . ."[45]

Hazlitt, as I shall point out more fully in Chapters IV and V, was aware of other practical implications of the ratio than this, but, at least for purposes of detraction, he was ready to identify Malthus's doctrine or Malthus's intent with the popular misunderstanding of the principle of population.[46] The degree to which Malthus was aware of the "law of diminishing returns" and his use of the arithmetical ratio to suggest it, have been matters of controversy and will be discussed in Chapter IV; but it should be pointed out here, as a difference between Wallace and Malthus that Hazlitt overlooked, that Malthus clearly recognizes at least one aspect of the "law," that is, the failure of additional tracts of land put under cultivation to reward the labor bestowed upon them to the extent that better land already under cultivation rewards the labor bestowed upon it, whereas Wallace, like Hazlitt, does not seem to differentiate among degrees of fertility, and implies, therefore, a relatively smaller return, for each unit of labor applied, only with regard to land already cultivated.[47]

---

[44] *Ibid.,* pp. 196-97.
[45] *Ibid.,* p. 195. My italics.
[46] Cf. *ibid.,* p. 197.
[47] A further difference between Wallace and Malthus is that Wallace does not use his theory of limited fertility to explain the establishment of marriage and private property, whereas Malthus calls these institutions "the most natural and obvious" means of minimizing population pressure. (*First Essay,* p. 199.)

HAZLITT'S DEFENSE OF SYSTEMS OF EQUALITY

The popular misconception of the ratios, and consequently of the function of vice and misery, is open to the charge of absurdity and inconsistency at many points where Malthus's own argument is not; but although Hazlitt, by identifying this misconception with Malthus's principle, unjustly ridicules the latter, his attack in the third letter shows fundamental differences between his and Malthus's explanation of human motives and how Hazlitt's explanation influenced his approach to population problems.

In it, as he promised in the first letter, Hazlitt proceeds to ridicule the *Essay* as contradictory, inconsistent, and absurd. First, he points out, although "the object of both the moralist and politician [had been] to diminish as much as possible the quantity of vice and misery in the world," Malthus in his first essay warned us that "in proportion as we attempt . . . to improve the condition of mankind, and lessen . . . the restraints of vice and misery, we thr[o]w down the only barrier that could protect us from . . . population." But in his second edition, Hazlitt finds, Malthus contradicts the first by saying "that virtue and happiness ought to be promoted by

---

Wallace, however, may have suggested Malthus's justification of these institutions. "The establishment of property in lands," he points out, "has been attended with many disadvantages; it seems indeed to have been one great source, not only of those calamities, but of those vices, which have been so sensibly felt, and so loudly complaind of in every age. At the same time, so far is it from appearing to have been necessary at the first constitution of society, that it seems rather to have been owing to accidents that it was first thought of, or that mankind consented to make such an experiment. Being ignorant and destitute of experience . . . and not foreseeing the evils to which the establishment of property would give occasion, they unfortunately had their first recourse to this expedient, instead of agreeing to an equitable distribution of labour, and to a community of goods. But if we consider their circumstances at that time, before any particular spots of the earth had been appropriated by individuals, the establishment of property does not appear to be *the most natural and obvious* scheme of promoting peace and union." (*Various Prospects of Mankind, Nature, and Providence,* pp. 109-10. My italics. Cf. Malthus's phrasing.)

Although questioning the wisdom of establishing property, Wallace adds that "in political questions it is easy to fall into errors, and to fancy things to be possible or advantageous, which, after a trial, would be found either impracticable or hurtful . . . . Perhaps, human affairs could not have been conducted according to a different system, or mankind made much wiser or happier than they have already been at certain periods of time." (*Various Prospects of Mankind, Nature, and Providence,* pp. 112-13.) This statement is followed immediately by Wallace's argument that a "perfect" society would be destroyed by population pressure.

every practicable means, and that the most effectual as well as desirable check to excessive population is moral restraint."[48] In the second place, since Malthus asks Godwin to name him any check "that does not fairly come under some form of vice and misery; except indeed the check of moral restraint,"[49] Hazlitt accuses him of trying to disprove Godwin's assertion "that vice and misery are not the only checks to population" simply by saying "that he himself truly has mentioned another check."[50] In the third place, Hazlitt takes up the greater part of the letter pointing out the absurdity of saying that a society of perfectly reasonable beings would be destroyed by unreasonable behavior.

The second of these "absurdities" is easily explained, for the context of the passage quoted from the *Thoughts,* which Hazlitt had evidently not bothered to look at, shows that Godwin had cited several checks as being neither vice, misery, nor moral restraint.[51] The first and third suggest important differences between Hazlitt and Malthus and, at the same time, similarities between Hazlitt and Godwin. The interpretation of the *Essay* implied here and the method of dealing with Malthus's arguments are much like Godwin's in his *Thoughts* and in the letter he wrote to Malthus shortly after the publication of the *Essay.*[52] Despite his rancor and his ridicule of Malthus's logic, Hazlitt does not, after all, object to the explanation of population pressure in the *Essay* but to the practical application proposed by Malthus, Whitbread, and others; in fact, in *The Spirit of the Age,* he thinks that Godwin "judged ill in endeavouring [in *Of Population*] to invalidate [Malthus's] principle, instead of confining himself to pointing out the misapplication of it.[53] In the *Thoughts,* however, Godwin praises not only "the spirit in which [the *Essay*] is written" and the author's disinterestedness, but also his "unquestion-

---

48 *Reply,* pp. 198-99.
49 *Essay* (2d ed.), Bk. III, chap. iii, pp. 383-84.
50 *Reply,* p. 200.
51 Godwin, *Thoughts,* pp. 62-63.
52 We do not have Godwin's letter to Malthus, but Malthus's reply indicates that it made the same criticism as that found in the *Thoughts.* Cf. C. K. Paul, *William Godwin, His Friends and Contemporaries* (London: Henry S. King & Co., 1876), I, 321-25.
53 "Mr. Malthus," *op. cit.,* p. 112.

able . . . addition to the theory of political economy";[54] he does "not attempt in the slightest degree to vitiate the great foundation of [Mr. Malthus's] theory," but confines himself "to the task of repelling his conclusions." He grants the ratios and the consequent necessity of some "constant and powerful check" upon population, but he refuses to believe that such checks must exist as to preclude "any important amelioration of the condition of mankind."[55] He undertakes to show, therefore, that the establishment and continuance of equalitarian society is, after all, *natural*—in that it is *possible* and at the same time in accord with that higher law which man as a reasonable being must recognize and obey.

Godwin, therefore, tries to show that poverty is not the "necessary" consequence of the principle of population, and like Hazlitt, he uses "necessary" to mean both "inescapable" and "expedient"; he interprets the *Essay* as maintaining not only the *inevitability* of vice and misery but also the *expediency* of preserving these checks, in their present extent, to protect society against something worse. Thus, he says, Malthus warns us that "no evil is more to be dreaded, than that we should have too little vice and misery in the world to confine the principle of population within its proper sphere."[56]

The expediency of vice and misery was frequently inferred by Malthus's critics, probably—according to Field—"from that part of [the *Essay*] that counseled the manner of action in charity and the provision for the poor."[57] Undoubtedly Malthus's opposition to poor relief seemed to Hazlitt to argue against "lessening the restraints of vice and misery," and in addition, as Hazlitt notes, the ratios suggested that population, if it increases at all, must inevitably increase faster and faster than subsistence; but with both Godwin and Hazlitt, it was also Malthus's opposition to economic equality that seemed to sanction the expediency of vice and misery. Both take Malthus's description of an equalitarian society collapsing in famine and disorder to be a warning against the re-

---

[54] *Thoughts*, pp. 10, 55-56. In *Of Population*, however, Godwin becomes as abusive as Hazlitt or any of the other critics.

[55] *Ibid.*, pp. 61-63.

[56] *Ibid.*, p. 59.

[57] Field, *op. cit.*, p. 28.

moval of vice and misery, for in the "perfect society" it was the absence of vice and misery, effected apparently by the equal distribution of food, that Malthus seems to represent as "offering extraordinary encouragements to population"—so extraordinary the number of inhabitants doubled twice in fifty years while the food increased in only an arithmetical progression.[58] Thinking of the power of the principle of population on one hand, says Godwin, and of the continual advance of "liberty" and "justice" on the other, people have been overfrightened by the prospect of "necessary" checks, although, despite this advance, the principle of population has never produced "those great and astonishing effects" predicted in the *Essay*.[59] Hazlitt, too, thinks of "improvement" as an approximation to the perfect society—involving not only a more equitable or "just" distribution of goods but also, as means to this end, more reasonable and virtuous behavior. And just as Godwin finds the *Essay* discouraging the advance of "liberty" and "justice," Hazlitt finds Malthus's warning against a community of goods inimical to any plan for more equitable distribution and to the correlative advance in reason and virtue. The "vice, misery, and madness," he argues, indicated by Malthus as "inseparable" from "a state of *unlimited* improvement, of perfect wisdom, virtue and happiness," would —if Malthus's argument were admitted—be an effectual bar to all limited improvement whatever."[60]

Hazlitt, it becomes evident, does not acknowledge the distinction that Malthus makes between methods of trying to lessen poverty, that is, between the kind of improvement suitable to "compound-beings" and that suitable to reasonable beings. Godwin, of course, based his reply upon the possibility of the latter kind. To show that the "perfect" society would not be subject to more and more vice and misery, Godwin argues that the prudential check, which operates in contemporary society to control vice and misery, would operate even more successfully in a society of rational beings.

It is true, the ill consequences of numerous family will not come so

---

58 *First Essay*, pp. 185-90.
59 *Thoughts*, pp. 68-70.
60 *Reply*, p. 206.

coarsely home to each man's individual interest as they do at present. It is true, a man in such a state of society might say, If my children cannot subsist at my expence, let them subsist at the expence of my neighbor. *But it is not in the human character to reason after this manner in such a situation.* The more men are raised above poverty and a life of expedients, the more decency will prevail in their conduct, and sobriety in their sentiments. Where everyone has a character, no one will be willing to distinguish himself by headstrong imprudence. Where a man possesses any reasonable means of pleasure and happiness, he will not be in a hurry to destroy his own tranquility or that of others by thoughtlessness.[61]

Malthus's reply to Godwin makes the distinction between methods of improvement that Hazlitt does not acknowledge. Malthus answered Godwin's letter a few months after the publication of the *Essay*[62] and then inserted a more elaborate refutation in his second edition. It was only to give warning against the "great political immorality" of trying to effect such a society, Malthus asserts in the second edition, that he predicted disaster: if the "great and astounding affects" have not been evident, it is because "in the past instance . . . has an attempt been made to establish such a system as Mr. Godwin's."[63] Furthermore, in both the letter and the second edition, Malthus argues that Godwin's admission of the necessity of prudence and his acceptance of the ratios partially removed the blame for misery from human institutions and placed it on man himself. Godwin would have replied, of course, that prudence, like benevolence, is one of the virtues natural to man; and that if his foresight were not unnaturally obscured by institutions, he would refrain from producing redundant population just as naturally as he would grant his neighbor's right to subsistence.

Malthus, however, does not grant the possibility of a society composed of completely disinterested beings. Although he, too, wishes to believe "that the present structure of society might be radically changed," he insists that there must always be, with the possible alternative of reverting to barbarism, "a class of proprietors and a class of labourers,

---

[61] *Thoughts,* p. 73.
[62] Paul, *op. cit.,* I, 321-25.
[63] *Essay* (2d ed.), Bk. III, chap. iii, pp. 382-83.

. . . the system of barter and exchange, and . . . the general moving principle of self-love." He does not grant that prudence could ever be practiced to the extent of so reducing the pressure of population on subsistence that this sort of structure would be unnecessary.[64] As Malthus explains explicitly in the second edition, we have no right to expect the future conduct of men with respect to abstinence from marriage to be much different from that in the past.[65] Therefore, possibilities of improvement must be considered with constant reference to a social structure like the present one. Now the prudential check "implies a foresight of difficulties; and this foresight almost necessarily implies a desire to remove them." On the level of contemporary society, then, how—except through "the interference of government, which I know you would reprobate as well as myself"—could this "natural and general desire" be kept from causing such competition as would preclude an equal division of labor and property?[66]

Therefore, by recommending moral restraint in his second edition as a means toward improvement, Malthus does not contradict his earlier argument that the condition of society must remain essentially unchanged. He still insists on the possibility of only *limited* improvement differing both in kind and in degree from that proposed by Godwin. Private property and marriage must be preserved to check the inclination toward idleness and propagation, and since these institutions insure inequality, society can no more approach Godwin's ideal than one parallel line can approach another.[67] Vice and misery are "necessary" in that, judging from past experience, the prudential check cannot prevent some pressure of population against subsistence, the pressure becoming evident in the poverty of the marginal class. These checks are not *expedient*,[68] but their

---

[64] Paul, *op. cit.*, I, 322-23.
[65] *Essay* (2d ed.), Bk. IV, chap. iii, pp. 504-05.
[66] Paul, *op. cit.*, I, 323-24.
[67] *First Essay*, pp. 281-82.
[68] ". . . I feel . . . mortified, that [Mr. Godwin] should think it a fair inference from my positions, that the political superintendents of a community are bound to exercise a paternal vigilance and care over the two great means of advantage and safety to mankind, misery and vice; and that no evil is more to be dreaded than that we should have too little of them in the world, to confine the principle of population within its proper sphere." (*Essay* [2d ed.], Bk. III, chap. iii, p. 381.)

diminution, through providing a greater share of food for the poor, should be attempted not by the practice of *benevolence* —that is, by public or private charity or by establishing a community of goods—but by making *self-love* enforce the prudential check—that is, by eliminating at least public charity and offering food only in return for labor.

Hazlitt, however, does not recognize Malthus's distinction between methods of trying to improve the condition of the poor. Malthus's "disciples," he points out, consider the ratios not only "as decisive against any philosophical scheme of perfectibility" but also "as proportionately inimical to any subordinate approximation to any such visionary perfection."[69] This identification of "any improvement" with "any subordinate approximation . . . to visionary perfection" may show simply Hazlitt's failure to follow Malthus's argument closely enough or more probably, his concern "not [for] Mr. Malthus's nonsense [itself], but [for] the opinion of the world respecting it . . .";[70] but also it is consistent with Hazlitt's attack on selfishness as an obstacle to improvement. Improvement, Hazlitt believes, depends on a benevolent interest in the poor and is prevented in a society where self-love is to be the "moving principle" of society. He does not consider man as a completely rational being, but, on the other hand, he does not make Malthus's sharp distinction between rational and "compound-beings." Like Malthus, he minimizes a calculation of consequences as a factor controlling human actions; but although he rejects the entirely reasonable behavior foreseen by Godwin as beyond man's capabilities, he thinks that control of sexual desire may be so increased by "habit" and "cultivation" that a disproportion between food and population will not be inevitable and that the "benevolence" of adequate relief, higher wages, or even a communism of goods would be more effectual in reducing poverty than abandoning relief in the hope that the poor would proportion their numbers to the available food.

Hazlitt's program for improvement can be discussed adequately only in connection with the later letters, but I wish

---

69 "An Examination of Mr. Malthus's Doctrines," *op. cit.*, p. 335.
70 *Reply*, p. 203.

to point out now that, although Hazlitt does not admit it, he and Malthus have the same *end* in view—the reduction of poverty—whereas they disagree only with regard to the *means* and *possible extent* of improvement.

Thinking of improvement in these terms and continually confusing Malthus's opposition to means as opposition to ends as well, Hazlitt is in a position to dismiss a great deal of the *Essay* as "contradictory" and "contrary to common sense," and as being without "order and connection" or "consistency of parts."[71] ". . . It will always be difficult," Hazlitt asserts at the beginning of the fourth letter, "to persuade the generality of mankind that a less degree of improvement is a good thing, though a greater would be a bad thing," but this is what "Mr. Malthus . . . endeavours formally to establish. . . ."[72] In the *Essay*, of course, there is not the absurdity Hazlitt would point out, for the "less degree" is that possible to "compound-beings," whereas the "greater" represents improvement possible only to rational beings and therefore not "bad" but inconceivable.

Similarly, in the third letter, Hazlitt "cannot agree with Mr. Malthus that [schemes of equality] would be *bad,* in proportion as they were *good;* . . . or that the true and only unanswerable objection against all such schemes is that very degree of *happiness,* virtue and improvement to which they are supposed to give rise." Malthus's answer to Godwin and to Condorcet's *Progrès de l'esprit humain,* therefore, is represented as a "complete piece of wrongheadedness" and a "strange perversion of reason."[73] Hazlitt offers Malthus the alternatives of (1) accepting the increased reasonableness, and consequent control of passion, that would be found in the perfect state or (2) granting that man's reason is so weak that such a state cannot be reached—and that consequently there is no point in crying up the dangers of reaching it. Although "a state of society in which everything will be subject to the control of reason" may for other reasons be considered "absurd, unnatural, or impracticable," it is the "grossest inconsistency"

---

[71] *Reply,* pp. 186-87, 201.
[72] *Ibid.,* pp. 207-08.
[73] *Ibid.,* pp. 200-01.

to object "that such a system would necessarily be proved abortive, because if reason should ever get this mastery over all our actions, we shall then be governed entirely by our physical appetites and our passions, without regard to consequences."[74] On the other hand, if Malthus maintains "that men will always be governed by the same gross mechanical motives that they are at present," he is still, Hazlitt insists, in an absurd position. "It is *very* idle to alarm the imagination by deprecating evils that must follow from the practical adoption of a particular scheme, yet to allow that we have no reason to dread those consequences, but because the scheme itself is impracticable."[75]

Wallace, much more than Malthus, is liable to the charge of absurdity on this score, and the applicability of Hazlitt's charge to the *Various Prospects* suggests once more his failure to distinguish between the contributions of Wallace and Malthus. Malthus, however, does not grant that reason could actually "get this mastery over all our actions"; Hazlitt is right in saying that Malthus granted "the desirableness of [Godwin's and Condorcet's] schemes,"[76] but he is wrong in interpreting the *Essay* as allowing their "practicability."[77] In fact, Malthus states explicitly that the equalitarian society whose overthrow he so vividly pictures could never have come into existence;[78] and in its hypothetical existence he peopled it not with rational beings but with compound ones. If he is "inconsistent," the "inconsistency" lies between *his* "perfect" society and Godwin's, but given the conditions that Malthus clearly states—a community of goods and compound beings—his argument assumes the familiar and consistent pattern recognizable throughout the *Essay*. But in rejecting Hazlitt's first alternative, must Malthus accept the second? Is he, then, "absurd" in "object[ing] to a system on account of the consequences which would follow if we were to suppose men to be actuated by entirely different motives and principles from

---

[74] *Ibid.*, p. 201.
[75] *Ibid.*, p. 203.
[76] *First Essay*, p. 7.
[77] *Reply*, p. 210.
[78] "The same causes in nature which would destroy it so rapidly, were it once established, would prevent the possibility of its establishment." (*First Essay*, p. 210. Cf. p. 175.)

what they are at present, and then . . . say[ing] that those consequences would necessarily follow, because men would never be what we suppose them"? In the first place, he is *not* supposing any change in men's motives (for his "perfect" society is not "consistent" with Godwin's); and in the second place, he believes that since men's motives will *not* change, any attempt to *approach* a communistic society would be dangerous. On the level of practical measures for improving the condition of the poor, the conditions of Malthus's "perfect" society— irrational beings and a communism of goods—are simulated, respectively, by the poor and such an arrangement as the Poor Laws: and the disastrous results of the "perfect" society correspond, with a difference only in *degree,* to the vice and misery caused by granting good otherwise than in exchange for labor. Insofar, therefore, as Malthus is "alarm[ing] the imagination by deprecating the evils that must follow from the practical adoption of a . . . scheme [of equality]," the "particular scheme"[79] actually put into practice would not be Godwin's communistic society in all its rationality or even this communistic society peopled, somehow, by irrational beings, but any *partial* communism of goods established as an attempted approach to Godwin's ideal.

Sixteen years later, in the *London Magazine* for October, 1823, De Quincey pointed out more accurately than Hazlitt had done, just where the "inconsistency" in Malthus's use of this argument lies, for he acknowledges that Malthus assumed the possibility of a perfect society not as something "practical" but only for the sake of argument—not as an *"absolute* truth" but as a "formal or logical truth"—but then became illogical by not holding to all the conditions of his assumption, thereby committing "the greatest logical oversight that has ever escaped any author of respectability." In a state of perfection such as assumed by Malthus, De Quincey asserts, men must have a clear view of the "fatal result" of overpopulation, but if the human will could not "nevertheless bring its own acts into harmony with reason and conscience . . . it must be in a most diseased state." Mr. Malthus, it is true, takes for granted "that no important change will ever take place in that

---

[79] *Reply,* p. 203. My italics.

part of human nature," but the assumption is not consistent with his agreement to argue "on the supposition that a state of perfection might be and actually was attained. . . . He agrees to suppose a perfect state; and at the same time he includes in his supposition the main imperfection of this world— viz. the diseased will of man."[80]

With respect to the following parts of the *Reply*, therefore, the first three letters, although they offer little or no constructive criticism, and often deal angrily and unfairly with both Malthus and his arguments, are especially important, respectively, for (1) showing Hazlitt's opposition to habitual selfishness and implying his explanation of human motives, (2) revealing his interpretation of the ratios and the line of argument it dictates, and (3) illustrating his method of ridiculing the *Essay* as "absurd" and "contradictory," and also suggesting the application of his psychological doctrine to the population problem.

---

[80] De Quincey, *op. cit.*, pp. 14-16.

CHAPTER IV

THE RATIOS

Although the personal abuse and the ridicule of Malthus's reasoning continue, the more constructive part of the *Reply* may be said to begin with Letter IV; for, to clear the road to improvement of the obstacles that he believes Malthus has put there, Hazlitt returns to the argument suggested at the end of the second letter and tries to explain the relation of population increase to the increase of subsistence.

Subsistence, Hazlitt points out, has the power of increasing, and sometimes does increase, in a geometrical rather than an arithmetical progression.[1] "Therefore," he continues, "it is not true as an abstract proposition, that of itself, or in the nature of the growth of the produce of the earth, food can only increase in the snail-pace progress of an arithmetical ratio, while population goes on at a swinging geometrical rate. . . ."

. . . Food keeps pace, or more than keeps pace, with population, while there is room to grow it in, and after that room is filled up, it does not go on, even in that arithmetical ratio—it does not increase at all, or very little. That is, the ratio, instead of being always true, is never true at all: neither before the soil is fully cultivated, nor afterwards.[2]

Similarly Hazlitt attacks the "practicality" or actuality of the geometrical ratio. This ratio, he argues, expresses only the "power" or *"unchecked tendency"* to increase, that is, "an abstract thing independent of circumstances, and . . . therefore always the same." On the contrary, the "real tendency [of population] to increase, . . . [its] actual, positive, practical tendency . . . *to increase,"* varies with the amount of food available for its support, and whether this tendency is expressible as an arithmetical or a geometrical ratio depends on how rapidly subsistence is increasing.[3] Just as subsistence

---

[1] *Reply,* pp. 197-98, 230. Cf. "An Examination of Mr. Malthus's Doctrines," *op. cit.,* p. 333.

[2] "An Examination of Mr. Malthus's Doctrines," *op. cit.,* p. 333.

[3] *Reply,* p. 220.

fails to realize its "power" of increasing geometrically when limited by the fertility or extent of the land, so must population, when subsistence is checked "by natural or artificial causes," be brought down to subsistence by the action of vice, misery, and moral restraint.[4]

Malthus does not deny that food, under certain circumstances, can increase geometrically; the arithmetical ratio represents simply the maximum rate of increase suggested by experience as probable in England and as applicable, therefore, to the "average" state of the earth, that is, to older countries where the land has already been cultivated to a considerable degree.[5] The great increase of food available in Europe during the nineteenth century and the accompanying growth of population may seem to render the arithmetical ratio and its limiting effect upon population as "impractical" as Hazlitt or any other critic could wish; but at least in relation to the time of the controversy the ratios still cannot be dismissed as merely "theoretical" or "supposititious."[6] As Field points out, the ratios "admirably stated the problem of population pressure" at the time of Malthus.[7] Whether or not the rate at which food was made available to the people of England in the late eighteenth and early nineteenth centuries was "artificially" retarded, there can be no doubt that it limited population growth to a rate well short of its potential one, for as more subsistence was made available, the number of people in Europe increased greatly.

This extremely rapid growth of population, far from proving that Malthus was wrong regarding the forces making for population growth in his day, bears out his chief contention. He was right in supposing that under the conditions prevailing in his day population would increase if more subsistence were available.[8]

Furthermore, regardless of the labor applied and improvement in technique, the food raised on any given piece of land

---

[4] *Ibid.*, pp. 230-31.
[5] *Essay* (2d ed.), Bk. I, chap. i, p. 7; Bk. III, chap. i, p. 357.
[6] Cf. *Gray versus Malthus*, pp. 3, 11, 58, and *passim;* Ensor, *op. cit.*, pp. 94-95; Godwin, *Of Population*, pp. 133-36, 480-81.
[7] *Op. cit.*, p. 20.
[8] Warren S. Thompson, *Population Problems* (2d ed.; New York: McGraw-Hill Book Company, Inc., 1935), p. 45.

—even though that piece of land be the whole world—must eventually be limited at least to the arithmetical rate of increase. Malthus's suggestion of the "law of diminishing returns" does not, perhaps, make sufficient allowance for factors that may suspend or temporarily control this law; but the point must eventually be reached, in the cultivation of land, at which production is no longer proportioned to the capital and labor applied to it. Thus, although the development of transportation and manufacturing made England by 1850 "definitely a food-importing country" and "for practical purposes . . . more than doubled the area and resources of Europe,"[9] the ratios still illustrate the "plain fact that the abstract potentiality of human increase cannot permanently be realized. . . ."[10]

In a review of Hazlitt's *Reply* and Ingram's *Disquisitions* in the *Edinburgh Review* it is pointed out, perhaps by Malthus himself, that the ratios imply not a necessarily increasing disparity between actual population and food but the tendency of population to increase as the availability of subsistence increases and the inability of population permanently to realize its power of increase.[11] Hazlitt does not question these "facts" but finds the reviewer's defense of Malthus consisting "in an adoption, point by point, of the principal objections and limitations, which have been offered to Mr. Malthus's system. . . ."

. . . With regard to the general principle of the disproportion between the power of increase in population, and in the means of subsistence, I have never in any instance called in question either of "these important and radical facts," which it is the business of Mr. M's work to illustrate. All that I undertook in the Reply to the Essay was to disprove Mr. Malthus's claim to the discovery of these facts, and to show that he had drawn some very false and sophistical conclusions from them, which do not appear in the article in the Review.[12]

This acknowledgment is implicit, at least, in the *Reply,* for by

---

[9] *Ibid.,* pp. 44-45.
[10] Field, *op. cit.,* p. 9, Cf. Henry Pratt Fairchild, *People. The Quantity and Quality of Population* (New York: Henry Holt and Company, 1939), pp. 100-05; Edward B. Reuter, *Population Problems* (2d ed. rev.; Chicago: J. B. Lippincott Company, 1937), pp. 170-71; Thompson, *op. cit.,* p. 46.
[11] Disquisitions on Population," *op. cit.,* p. 469.
[12] Notes to the *Political Essays,* pp. 409-10.

pointing out that the geometrical and arithmetical ratios are not fixed in nature, that population and subsistence do not inexorably advance at increasingly different rates, Hazlitt does not remove the problem of the ratios, but merely restates it. He grants (1) that however complete the utilization of the world's resources might be, the biologically possible increase of population could not permanently be realized,[13] and (2) that conditions were such in England and other European countries (a) that this rate fell far short of realization and (b) that the availability of more food would increase population.

He does not deny a disparity between actual and potential population and that population, therefore, has a *tendency* to excess; but in order to prove that the relative amount of vice and misery contingent upon increased production and population will not be greater but probably less, he denies that this tendency exists in the literal sense suggested by the ratios. Since the "actual, positive, practical tendency in population *to increase*," that is, the actual growth in numbers, changes with available subsistence, "for that very reason," Hazlitt believes, "its tendency *to excess* is always the same . . . in consequence of the absolute increase in population."[14] It is true that "the excess of the power [of population to increase] over the means of subsistence . . . is greater as we advance,"[15] but unless this "excess" were translated into *only* the checking action of "*actual* vice and misery (not foreseen, but felt),"[16] the "tendency to excess" is not proportionably greater. Actually, the "excess" does not manifest itself as a number of people born only to be starved out of existence, for, according to "all we know of facts and human nature,"[17] people "will submit to be *pinched,* but not to be *starved.* . . ."[18] It is a

---

[13] *Reply*, pp. 197-98.
[14] *Ibid.,* p. 220.
[15] *Ibid.,* p. 223.
[16] *Ibid.,* p. 227.
[17] *Ibid.*
[18] *Ibid.,* p. 229. In the *Reply* Hazlitt, like Malthus in the early editions of the *Essay,* incautiously represents the "excess" in numerical terms (p. 220), but the passages I have quoted indicate that he thought of it as existing only "morally." Hazlitt makes this concept clear in the *Political Essays,* where he writes: ". . . The population . . . never can or does exceed the means of subsistence in a literal sense; and the tendency to exceed it in a moral sense, that is, so as

"degree of moral restraint," therefore, "operat[ed] on" by a "degree of actual vice and misery" that brings the population down to the level of subsistence.[19] The motives to resist the sexual passion may vary from "very slight" ones to the pressure of "absolute famine."

But in no case unless we suppose man to be degraded to the condition of the brutes, will this principle be so low and weak as to have no effect at all, so that no apprehension of the last degree of wretchedness, as the consequence, would take off or abate the edge of appetite. There is therefore always a point at which the excess ceases. . . .[20]

That is, the "excess," or a certain amount of actual vice and misery, is limited at the point where people responding to the "difficulty of providing for [the] support [of a family]," exercise prudential restraint to bring population down to the level of subsistence.[21]

Malthus, of course, despite incautious representations of population in numerical terms, does not hold that, as the production of food increases, there is an increasingly large number of people for whom no food can be provided. And he recognizes, as well, that the "excess," in terms of vice and misery, is limited by the exercise of the prudential check. In other words, both Hazlitt and Malthus, and other critics who grant the operation of the prudential check,[22] consider population as pressing on what modern economists and sociologists call the "level" or "standard" or "plane" of living, rather than directly on subsistence. According to Hazlitt, a certain level of living is maintained because, for each person, there is a "degree of wretchedness" even less pleasant in prospect

---

to destroy the comforts and happiness of society, and occasion vice and misery, does not depend on the actual population . . . but solely on the greater or less degree of moral restraint . . ." ("An Examination of Mr. Malthus's Doctrines," *op. cit.*, pp. 334-35.)

[19] *Reply*, p. 231. Hazlitt does not, like Malthus, explicitly limit "moral restraint" to the postponement of marriage, but I have found no evidence that he uses the term to include contraception.

[20] *Ibid.*, p. 228.

[21] *Ibid.*, p. 223.

[22] Jarrold, *op. cit.*, pp. 52-56, 251-52; [Weyland], *A Short Inquiry*, pp. 34-37; Ingram, *op. cit.*, pp. 4-5, 30-35, 100-01, 117-19, and *passim;* Grahame, *op. cit.*, p. 198; *Gray versus Malthus*, pp. 94-95, 124, 143-44, 163, and *passim;* Ensor, *op. cit.*, pp. 145-48, 487-88.

than the denial of sexual gratification[23]—that is, there is a command of goods which he will not relinquish in order to marry or to increase the size of his family—and whenever that degree seems imminent, he will resort to the prudential check to prevent, if he can, its realization. Malthus, too, considered population to press on the level of living rather than directly on subsistence. The "ultimate check" or "want of food," he says, "is never the immediate check, except in cases of actual famine." The immediate check, he adds, consists "in all those customs, and all those diseases which seem to be generated by a scarcity of the means of subsistence; and all those causes, independent of scarcity, whether of a moral or physical nature, which tend prematurely to weaken and destroy the human frame."[24] The preventive check, as one of the "customs . . . generated by . . . scarcity," interposes a protective layer between population and the means of subsistence, so that the "ultimate check" and even "those diseases . . . generated by . . . scarcity," may have little or no effect. Whole groups may, in this way, be kept well above the level of starvation.[25] Malthus and Hazlitt seem to agree, then, that although the growth of population is ultimately limited by the amount of food it can command, the prudential check usually limits the size of the family at a point where income that would otherwise be used to obtain a maximum amount of food is diverted, in part, to obtain more expensive foods or other products.

---

[23] Until dealing with very recent population phenomena, Professor Fairchild believes, it is not necessary to distinguish between "the desire for mating" and "the desire for offspring." (*Op. cit.*, pp. 129-30.)

[24] *An Essay on the Principle of Population* . . . (3d ed.; London: J. Johnson, 1806), Vol. I, Bk. I, chap. ii, p. 15.

[25] *Essay* (2d ed.), Bk. II, chap. ix, pp. 300-01; Bk. II, chap. xi, p. 351. Cf. *Essay* (3d ed.), Vol. II, Bk. IV, chap. x, pp. 452-58.

CHAPTER V

HAZLITT'S CASE AGAINST INSTITUTIONS

Having questioned the "naturalness" of the arithmetical ratio, the critics usually proceed to specify institutions that limit production or prevent more equitable distribution and to conclude that vice and misery, therefore, are not "necessary." Hazlitt argues that (1) since, in some of their forms, the checks of vice and misery can be traced to other causes than the lack of food and since these causes are removable, (2) since the insufficiency of food may be remedied by producing more food and distributing it more equitably, and (3) since a reduction in the vice and misery resulting from both the lack of food and other causes will at the same time encourage the prudential check—since, as experience shows, all these propositions are true, vice and misery are not (1) unavoidable or (2) expedient to prevent overpopulation.

After pointing out that vice and misery have other causes than scarcity of provisions[1]—a concession that Malthus of course readily granted—Hazlitt asserts that the distress resulting from insufficient food is more capable of human regulation than Malthus admits. Given some limitation of the food-producing capacity short of supplying the potential increase of population, food must be the ultimate check and, as Hazlitt admits, this limitation must eventually be felt if population keeps on increasing. Furthermore, Hazlitt agrees, if for any reason the food available to a society is curtailed short of supplying the potential increase in numbers, the lack of food must still be the ultimate check to population, although its impact may be cushioned by the prudential check.[2] But the "necessity" of the limitation or curtailment at any one time and its effect upon the level of living offer still further grounds for dispute. In the fifth letter, therefore, Hazlitt calls attention to the "human institutions [which] aggravate instead of mitigating the *necessary* evils of population."

---

[1] *Reply*, pp. 257-58, 265-66, 277-80.
[2] *Ibid.*, pp. 197-98.

We have a sufficient specimen [cited in the *Essay* itself] of the effects of bad government, of bad laws, of the worse execution of them, of feeble and selfish policy, of wars and commotions, or of diseases probably occasioned for the most part by the numbers of people who are huddled together in dirt and poverty in the great towns in the manner we have seen—in altering the natural proportion between the produce of the soil, and the maintenance of the inhabitants; in wantonly diminishing the means of subsistence by a most unjust and unequal distribution of them; in diverting the produce of industry from its proper channels, in drying up its sources, in causing the stagnation of all the motives and principles which animate human life, in destroying all confidence, independence, hope, cheerfulness, and manly exertion, in thwarting the bounties of nature by waste, rapacity, extortion and violence, and spreading want, misery, and desolation in their stead.[3]

Believing that the motivating power of even "pride, avarice, and indolence"[4] might be reduced by habit and cultivation, Hazlitt denies the inevitability of private property; but it is indicative of his "preoccupation with bringing down the revolutionary philosophy to the level of human nature" that he should be more concerned with equalizing distribution under a system of private property than with establishing common ownership. Malthus, Hazlitt reminds us, lays the evil of inequality directly to private property, which he supposes to result "necessar[il]y . . . [from] laws inherent in our nature"; but even "the established administration of property," says Hazlitt, and the evils attendant upon it "would be no longer necessary" if "sloth and rapacity . . . could be completely subdued, so that no one would refuse his share in the common labour, or endeavor to take unfair advantage of others either by force or fraud. . . ."[5]

Such a change [Hazlitt adds in a footnote] would not require the perfect subjugation, or rather annihilation of these passions, or perfect virtue, in the literal sense. . . . It might as well be pretended that no man could ever keep his fingers off bank-notes, or pay his debts, who was not perfectly honest. In neither case is there required anything more than such a superiority in one set for [of?] motives over another, from pride, habit, example, opinion, &c. as just to incline the balance.[6]

---

3 *Ibid.*, p. 257.
4 *Ibid.*, p. 250.
5 *Ibid.*, p. 251.
6 *Ibid.*, p. 251, n.

At the end of the footnote, however, Hazlitt confesses that he "meddle[s] with these questions only as things of idle speculation." He does not urge either the communism of goods or the anarchy of *Political Justice,* but examines the existing forms of society for the effect of government on production and distribution.

The function of law and government described by Hazlitt in his "Project for a New Theory of Civil and Criminal Legislation" is to limit the freedom of individuals in the pursuit of their inclinations, but this right of the government can arise only "from the necessity of maintaining the equal rights of every one, and of opposing force to force in case of any violent and unwarrantable infringement of them."[7] A "right," according to Hazlitt, is simply "that which is thought [good and useful] by the individual, and which has the sanction of the will as such,"[8] but when the individual lives "among a number of equally selfish and self-willed beings," the principle of self-interest limits his "rights" to those to which "he can lay claim, [and simultaneously] allow . . . the same latitude and allowance to others."[9] Were men completely reasonable beings, the limitation of individual rights in society in order to preserve equal rights for all could be left, as Godwin believes, to "moral justice, which implies only an appeal to reason," but in "a real state of things," "political justice, which implies an appeal to force" must assign "the limits of . . . individual rights in society. . . ."[10] But the use of force by a government must not go beyond that required by "political justice," for government "has no right to trench upon the liberty or rights of the individuals its members, except as these last are . . . forfeited . . . by interfering with and destroying one another. . . ."[11]

A "tyrannical government," then, as opposed to a "free government" is one extending its control beyond the necessities of "political justice." Tyranny, Hazlitt points out in the

---

[7] "Project for a New Theory of Civil and Criminal Legislation," *Literary and Political Criticism,* XIX, 305.
[8] *Ibid.,* p. 303.
[9] *Ibid.,* p. 304.
[10] *Ibid.*
[11] *Ibid.,* p. 305.

Reply, may be traced, as in Rome, to the desire for luxury,[12] or perhaps to "men of shining abilities,"[13] rather than to the inherent limitation of subsistence, but everywhere, especially as it infringes on the right of property, it has discouraged cultivation, and therefore population, and made for extremes of wealth and poverty. The right of a man in "a state of . . . solitary independence . . . to all he can lay his hands on"[14] must be limited in deference to the rights of others in a society and further curtailed to meet the expense of government; but for "moral and final causes" labor must be considered as giving the right to property, "because if one enjoyed what another had produced, there would be nothing but idleness and rapacity" and also because "the labour undergone, or the time lost, is entitled to an equivalent, *caeteris manentibus*";[15] and where the government restricts one's right to the product of his labor more than the expense of "keep[ing] the peace"[16] requires, in order to satisfy the greed of the rulers, depopulation and poverty result.[17]

Having shown that morality and happiness vary with other factors than the food supply and that the food supply and its distribution vary with circumstances controllable by man, Hazlitt must prove that a higher degree of morality or the increased availability of food will raise the level of living rather than lower it. He tries to show, therefore, that the removal of vice and misery will tend not to increase but to confine the tendency to excess and that, consequently, the retention of those evils is not "necessary," or expedient to prevent worse evils.

Hazlitt continually objects that Malthus, instead of "adopt-[ing] the necessarian maxim that men will be always the same while circumstances continue," makes the mistake of "insist-[ing] upon it that they will be always the same, whether the circumstances are the same or not." Thus, in attacking Godwin,

---

12 *Reply,* pp. 266-68.
13 *Ibid.,* pp. 276-77.
14 "Project for a New Theory of Civil and Criminal Legislation," *op. cit.,* p. 317.
15 *Ibid.,* p. 318.
16 "What Is the People?" (concluded), *op. cit.,* p. 275.
17 For Hazlitt's illustrations from history cf. *Reply,* pp. 225, 253-57, 264, 271-79.

Malthus succeeds only in showing what would be the consequences of the "perfect" society "if no such state or society really existed, but if everything remained just as it is at present."[18] And in what Hazlitt supposes to be his deprecation of "improvement," he succeeds, Hazlitt would say, only in showing what would be the consequences of improvement if no improvement had taken place. Thus, as we have seen in examining the fourth letter, Hazlitt believes that, under the conditions necessary for securing more food, man's mastery over his passions must be strengthened and that the higher level of living accompanying the increased production and more equitable distribution of food is due to the greater responsiveness of the prudential check to the danger of losing one's command of goods. In the fifth letter, in order to show the consequences of moral and economic improvement, Hazlitt explains more fully the conditions that affect "moral restraint."

Like other critics, Hazlitt attacks Malthus's analogy between hunger and the sexual passion. The latter is not a matter of "mere physical necessity" but, as the number of chaste unmarried women indicates, something influenced by "reason, or imagination, or habit. . . ."[19] Obviously, "moral causes," by which Hazlitt seems to imply a calculation of consequences plus the motivating force of habitually cultivated affections, play a part in regulating the sexual passion.[20]

---

18 *Ibid.,* pp. 286-87.

19 *Ibid.,* pp. 234-35.

20 *Ibid.,* p. 235. Denying the "necessity" of sexual intercourse gives Hazlitt an opportunity to employ the "flowery" and "descripti[ve]" style mentioned in the "Advertisement" to the *Reply* and to "amus[e]" his readers with some "personal observations." (*Ibid.,* p. 179.) Malthus, Hazlitt admits, seems never to have heard of or felt such passions as "anger, pride, avarice, sloth, drunkenness, envy, [and] revenge, . . . for he passes them over as trifles beneath the notice of a philosopher . . . . But the women are *the devil.*—The delights and torments of love no man, he tells us, ever was proof against: there all our philosophy is useless; and reason but an empty name . . . . The smiles of a fair lady are to him irresistible; the glimpse of a petticoat throws him into a flame; and all his senses are up in arms, and his heart fails within him, at the very name of love. His gallantry and devotion to the fair sex know no bounds; and he not only answers for himself, but undertakes to prove that all men are made of the same combustible materials. His book reminds one of the title of the old play, 'All for love, or the world well lost.'" (*Ibid.,* p. 242.) But this "combustibility," Hazlitt protests, is not constant: it varies with the manners of the age. Women's clothes in the "time of the Spectator"—"the counterfeit shapes, the stiff stays, and enormous hoops"—"repressed" the "greedy eye and rash hand of licentiousness," but now "young ladies" are "moving pictures of lust and nakedness, against which the greasy imaginations of grooms and porters may rub themselves, running the

Since the "command over passion" is apparently increased with a higher level of morality in a country, since, for instance, it is evident that it existed to a higher degree in a time like that of Cromwell than among "the young courtiers of the following reign,"[21] continued immorality is not made expedient by the principle of population.[22] Nor does the need for moral restraint sanction those institutions that "keep population down infinitely below the level to which it might rise by a proper encouragement of agriculture, and the methods of industry by which population is supported" or "those institutions which favour the greatest disparity of conditions, the extremes of poverty and the extremes of luxury. . . ."[23] On the other hand, it appears that "the principle of moral restraint is likely to operate with most effect" in "those states or communities, where the greatest equality prevails, [and] which maintain the greatest number of inhabitants."[24]

In the "Extracts" Hazlitt specifies one form of tyranny that makes for extremes of inequality in England. He does not, as might be expected from part of the fifth letter, blame private property, but, rather, he attacks the abuse of power derived from its possession. He approaches the problem, as usual, by maintaining that the vice and misery entailed by unequal distribution is not "necessary" to control population. As far as *"the principle of population . . . alone"* is concerned, Hazlitt believes, not "benevolent and perfect wisdom" but simply "self-love, and a little common sense" will serve as the "moving principles" for a "state of practical equality, admitting neither poverty nor riches."[25] Hazlitt is not, of course,

---

gauntlet of the saucy looks and indecent sarcasms of the boys in the street, staring at every ugly fellow, leering at every handsome man, and throwing out a lure for every fool . . . ." (*Ibid.,* p. 281.) In contrast with Malthus's susceptibility, however, Hazlitt's own "notions of this passion" have remained "temperate" and "tractable," perhaps because he "never fell in love but once; and then it was with a girl who always wore her handkerchief pinned tight round her neck, with a fair face, gentle eyes, a soft smile, and cool auburn locks." (*Ibid.,* p. 283.)

21 *Ibid.,* p. 241.

22 *Ibid.,* pp. 236-41. Thus Hazlitt suggests what Field calls "a socialization of the preventive check by a diffused spirit of continence which may characterize a period and in effect reduce the passion between the sexes that Malthus assumed to be constant." (*Op. cit.,* p. 41.)

23 *Reply,* p. 248.

24 *Ibid.,* pp. 248 ff.

25 *Ibid.,* p. 305.

contradicting his earlier insistence upon "benevolence" or "disinterestedness" as essential to "improvement," for he relies on this virtue to bring about the condition in which self-love may control the tendency to excess. He is not "enter[ing] into the general structure, foundation, or purposes of civil society" —which presumably depend on more than "self-love, and a little common sense"—but "examin[ing] the question only as a branch of political economy, or as it relates to the physical sustenance of mankind, which is the point of view in which Mr. Malthus has treated it."[26] That is, given security in the possession of certain rights, society can depend on the self-love of its members to prevent a shortage of food for any class, but granting the poor that security requires the disinterestedness of the ruling class.[27]

Malthus, Hazlitt continues, has discovered only "that it would be necessary in the progress of society, in order to stave off the evils of population, to make a regulation, that every man should be obliged to work for a subsistence, and to provide for his own children."[28] It is not true that "inequality of conditions must necessarily follow" the establishment of property and marriage and that the laborer, therefore, has a right to no more food than the subsistence or less-than-subsistence wage that the proprietor may choose to give him in exchange for his labor. Malthus thinks that those "born after the division of property" would have to depend, for subsistence, on the "fund appropriated for the maintenance of labour," which is "the aggregate quantity of food possessed by the owners of the land beyond their own consumption," and that, to make for as favorable proportion as possible between the workers and the wages fund, each worker should be required to support his own family.[29] The principle of population may make it expedient, Hazlitt agrees, that the food allowed the worker and his family should be only in exchange for his labor, but it does not follow that a man "has no claim of *right* to the smallest portion of food"[30] beyond that which

---

[26] *Ibid.*
[27] *Ibid.*, pp. 250, 344, and *passim.*
[28] *Ibid.*, pp. 305–06.
[29] *First Essay*, pp. 194–207.
[30] *Essay* (2d ed.), Bk. IV, chap. vi, p. 531. Malthus's italics. Quoted in *Reply*, p. 312.

society *as it is constituted at present* will give him for his labor. Hazlitt distinguishes, therefore, between the amount of food a laborer can actually obtain in contemporary society and the amount he could and should be allowed within the limitation of "abstract rights" imposed by the principle of population. To combat the dangers of idleness and overpopulation, it is only *"necessary"* that a man's "abstract right [to an equal share of the produce of the earth] be clogged with the condition that he should work for his share of it," so that his and his family's share shall be proportioned to his labor.[31] The right of private property as limited by this condition would be simply "a right in anyone to cultivate a piece of land . . . and a right at the same time to prevent any one else from cultivating it, or reaping the produce."[32] The right to the labor of others and its produce would not have to accompany the right of property; for, as far as the principle of population is concerned, the laborer could still be allowed "as much of the additional produce of the ground as he himself had really *added* to it."[33] The difference between the actual amount of food for which a man can exchange his labor and the amount he produces is not, therefore, necessary as a means of increasing his industry and prudence—unless it could be proved that a lower standard of living is more favorable to the exercise of these virtues. As Malthus himself acknowledges, however, and as experience shows, an acquaintance "with comfort and decency" does more than wretchedness to make a man industriousness and prudent.[34]

Nor is the right to subsistence limited "naturally," as Malthus believes, by the proportion of laborers to the amount of food left over from consumption by the rich. Malthus's argument that the limited produce of the earth reduces the laborer's claim to the amount of food he can exchange his labor for, proves only that "the right of subsistence or one man's right to live is only limited by its interfering with the right of others to live. . . . But it is not the question whether the proprietor should starve himself in order that the labourer

---

31 *Reply*, pp. 305-06.
32 *Ibid.*, p. 310.
33 *Ibid.*, p. 311.
34 *Ibid.*, pp. 308, 312, 314, and *passim*.

may live; but whether the proprietor has a right to live in extravagance and luxury, while the labourer is starving."[35] The "natural level" of wages hailed by Malthus as "expressing the relation between the supply of provisions, and the demand for them" and "the wants of the society respecting population"[36] has no "relation to real plenty or want."[37] The amount of food kept by the rich and the proportion remaining for the laborers is not, as Malthus would have us believe, "unalterable and one of the laws of nature," but "any arbitrary division of the produce of the ground, which the rich find it convenient to make, and which the poor are forced to take up with as better than nothing."[38] This distribution is not a "question of right any more than it is a question of expediency, but a question of power on one side, and of necessity on the other."[39] As long as the laborers are paid out of the produce of their own labor, they have as much right as the proprietor in establishing their wage, for the worker's "right to his liberty is just as good as [the owner's] right to [his] property."[40] Hazlitt "contend[s, therefore,] that the mass of the labouring community have always a right to *strike,* to demand what wages they please; the least that they can demand is enough to support them and their families; and the real contest will be between the aversion of the rich to labour, and of the poor to famine."[41] But regardless of the proportion between their numbers and the amount of food he and his fellow-laborers produce, the laborer is never free to exercise his right of refusing to "exchange his labour, without receiving a *sufficient* quantity of food in return,"[42] because "the right of the proprietor to exact the labour of others on what terms he chuses, is seconded by a kind of power, which has very little connection with the power of the earth to bring forth no more produce."[43] For although "the legislature assumes a right to prevent com-

---

[35] *Ibid.,* p. 318.
[36] *Essay* (2d ed.), Bk. III, chap. v, p. 406. Quoted in *Reply,* p. 331.
[37] *Reply,* p. 332.
[38] *Ibid.,* pp. 332-33.
[39] *Ibid.,* p. 312.
[40] *Ibid.,* p. 315.
[41] *Ibid.*
[42] *Ibid.,* p. 318. Hazlitt has substituted *"sufficient"* for Malthus's "ample." Cf. *First Essay,* p. 206.
[43] *Reply,* p. 318.

binations of the poor to keep themselves above want, . . .
they *disclaim* any right to meddle with monopolies of corn,
or other combinations *in the regular course of trade,* by which
the rich and thriving endeavor to grind the poor."[44] Hazlitt,
therefore, denies that "the period when the number of men
surpass their means of subsistence, has long since arrived,"[45]
for institutions keep population "below the level not only of
the possible, but of the *actual* means of subsistence or produce
of the earth."[46]

On the other hand, if the share kept by the rich were
limited, so that the share remaining to the laborers could actually be proportioned to their needs by industry and restraint
and were not always monopolized by the rich, the extremes
of wealth and poverty could be avoided, despite the institutions of private property and marriage. If Malthus really
meant, as "in one place" he seems to mean, only "to secure to
the rich their original right," which is to reserve a certain
share of the produce for their own use; and to prevent their
being driven out of house and home by the poor, under pre-
tence of population," Hazlitt would have no quarrel with
him. If, for instance, the proprietors kept or were granted
only "what is necessary for their own immediate consumption," even without working for it, the "difference in the advantages which the rich have over the poor" would be "almost
imperceptible. . . ."

In this case, it is evident, that "no man would be forced to exchange
his labour without receiving an ample quantity of food in return." At
this rate the laborer would be as rich, only not so idle as the proprietor.
. . . [The productions of labour] would in fact be a common fund
divided equally between the rich and the poor. . . .[47]

---

44 *Ibid.,* p. 319.
45 *Essay* (2d ed.), Bk. III, chap. i, p. 357.
46 *Reply,* p. 291.
47 *Ibid.,* pp. 320-21.

CHAPTER VI

HAZLITT'S DEFENSE OF THE POOR LAWS

Having shown that the workers' rights are curtailed by the power of the rich and having defended the right to strike, Hazlitt does not demand the repeal of the Combination Laws, which since 1800 had forbidden the laborers the right to organize, but attacks the facility of combination among the proprietors only to show, in contradiction to the *Essay*, that as long as this power continues, the withdrawal of relief will harm rather than benefit society. It seems that a change in the Combination Laws would have gone more directly to what Hazlitt considers the root of the difficulty; but of course it is Malthus to whom Hazlitt is replying, and it is the issue of the Poor Laws and not that of the Combination Laws that Malthus raised.

PROBABLE RESULTS OF WITHDRAWING RELIEF

Hazlitt believed that "improvement" should go beyond a system of parochial relief, but because the issue raised by Malthus and his disciples was the withdrawal of relief and because Hazlitt believed that revoking the Poor Laws would delay improvement by degrading the poor still further and by further hardening the hearts of the rich, the *Reply* and the *Political Essays* are primarily concerned with defending these laws. The "public mind," Hazlitt writes, has been infused with a prejudice against the poor, and while the poor are so "despised," he is "almost convinced that any serious attempt to better the[ir] condition . . . will be ineffectual."[1] The *Essay* has only strengthened "the habitual meanness and selfishness of our nature," and until reform can be undertaken in the spirit of disinterestedness necessary to success, our "only object" must be "to gain time."[2] The continuance of poor relief, a "corrective"[3] already established, appears to Hazlitt

---

[1] *Reply,* p. 182.
[2] *Ibid.*
[3] "Project for a New Theory of Civil and Criminal Legislation," *op. cit.,* p. 319.

to be the best way of gaining time against the day of greater benevolence. Similarly, although Hazlitt again argues for "the right of combination among journeymen and others,"[4] in still other essays he would grant the poor a larger share of food, not through higher wages, but by means of "a tax laid upon [pleasure- and coach-horses] directly, to defray the expense of the poor rates, and to suspend the operation of Mr. Malthus's geometrical and arithmetical ratios."[5]

The power of the rich, Hazlitt argues in the *Reply*, is to blame for the evils that Malthus traces to the Poor Laws. If a man could count on industry and moral restraint to improve his lot, or even to maintain a decent standard of living, he would be industrious and prudent; but when he has been emotionally and intellectually degraded by misery and the hopelessness of ever rising above it, he cannot be expected to make the same effort to control his inclinations. Malthus, Hazlitt insists, "confounds the cause with the effect."[6] ". . . That carelessness and want of frugality observable among the poor [and noted by Mr. Malthus], so contrary to the disposition generally to be remarked among petty tradesmen and small farmers,"[7] arises not from the increase in poor rates but from "the difference in their situations, from the greater hardships imposed upon the labouring part of the community, from their different prospects in life, and the little estimation in which they are held."[8] If the poor live "from hand to mouth," it is because "they have no hopes of living in any other way."[9] Malthus's proposal, therefore, "does not go to the root of the evil. . . ." Hazlitt thinks that "it would be well, if [the Poor Laws] could be got rid of, consistently with humanity and justice," but this would not be possible "in the present state of things and other circumstances remaining as they are."[10] As long as the rich have the power to engross as much

---

4 *Ibid.*, p. 309.
5 "Speeches on the Distresses of the Country, by Mr. Western and Mr. Brougham" (concluded), *Political Essays*, VII, 113. Cf. "Outlines of Political Economy," *Literary and Political Criticism*, XIX, 284-85.
6 *Reply*, p. 355.
7 *Essay* (2d ed.), Bk. III, chap. vi, pp. 410-11. Quoted in *Reply*, p. 337.
8 *Reply*, p. 337.
9 *Ibid.*, pp. 337-38.
10 *Ibid.*, p. 355.

food as they wish or, in other words, to drive wages down to the subsistence level or even lower, the withdrawal of poor relief would not have the effects that Malthus foresaw but would (1) further encroach upon the poor man's "right to subsistence,"[11] (2) so affect the "moral sensibility" of both rich and poor that improvement would be out of the question,[12] and (3) increase tyranny and despotism, so that a violent reaction would be more, rather than less, probable.[13]

EFFECTS OF THE POOR LAW OF 1834

Obviously it is impossible to say what the results of Malthus's plan would have been. The *Essay* influenced the restrictive Poor-Law legislation of 1818 and 1819, and the New Poor Law of 1834, which prohibited allowances and required the able-bodied pauper to earn his relief in a workhouse, was supported by Malthusian arguments; but some provision for the care of the poor remained. The respective roles of selfishness and disinterestedness in improving the condition of the working classes since the early nineteenth century can hardly be indicated, but that one or more of the other factors mentioned by Hazlitt would have interfered with the success of Malthus's plan does not seem unlikely. The power of the employer to determine wages has been less effectually controlled by admonitions like Malthus's than by strikes; the prudential check has had a negligible effect among depressed classes; and people denied bread have continued to rebel.

The New Poor Law, although not a full application of Malthus's principles, and although enforced under conditions different from those at the time of the *Reply,* provides some means for judging the accuracy of Hazlitt's predictions. This Act was both conceived and administered according to the principles of political economy, although more particularly Bentham's than Malthus's. The lack of prudential restraint still figures in the arguments supporting the Bill, but since the demand for Irish labor proved that population in England was

11 *Ibid.,* pp. 328-35.
12 *Ibid.,* pp. 314, 339, 340, 344, 360.
13 *Ibid.,* pp. 350-60.

not excessive, the emphasis shifts to securing freedom for the movement of labor and restoring the self-respect and industriousness that pauperism had destroyed.[14] The Act required, in addition to granting only indoor relief, that the condition of the pauper in the workhouse be made less attractive than that of the poorest laborer not on relief; that, in order to give labor more mobility, settlement be granted on fewer conditions; that in order to discourage population, illegitimate children be chargeable to the mother; and that three commissioners in London administer the Law. The commissioners were given not only the negative task of making life in the workhouse less attractive than self-support, but were entrusted with the education and apprenticeship of pauper children. They also sought to improve workhouses by providing separate wards for different classes of paupers, and organized emigration from crowded districts to less populous ones and even out of the country. In the areas into which the country was divided to effect these reforms more readily, the Law was administered by authorities elected, although under a system of plural voting, by all the ratepayers.

According to the report of the Poor Law Commissioners, the new law had, at least partially, the effect that Malthus had hoped to secure through his plan. It is reported to have raised the moral standard and consequently to have improved the economic position of the poorer classes.

The agricultural labourers were drinking less, and there had been a marked decrease in the number of public houses which had reached its height in 1830 and the years immediately following. More money was being placed in the savings-banks, and friendly societies were increasing their membership every year. And if in the southern counties the supply of labour was perhaps in excess of the demand, the act of 1834 empowered the commissioners to transport the superfluous labourers to districts where the demand was greater. They made use of their power and sent unemployed agricultural labourers—certainly a very few, some five thousand in all—to colonise Australia and New Zealand. They sent a far larger number to the Lancashire factories where they suddenly

---

14 Élie Halévy, *A History of the English People, 1830-1841*, trans. E. I. Watkin (New York: Harcourt, Brace & Co., n.d.), pp. 123-24; Nicholls, *op. cit.*, II, 281, 282-84; Hansard, *Parliamentary Debates*, 3d series, XXV (1834), 220.

found themselves in receipt of wages, twice or thrice the amount they had been earning on the farms of Sussex or Devonshire.[15]

The New Poor Law, nevertheless, was not popular among the people.[16] In its third year, according to the Poor Law Commissioners' report, "the new machinery and principles of relief . . . were tried" by a particularly severe winter and an epidemic of influenza among the laboring classes. "The fourth year was distinguished by extensive reverses in trade, and severe depression in the manufacturing districts, which threw out of employment for a time the greater proportion of the labouring population of several manufacturing towns; and this fifth year has been one of scarcity of food, and consequent high prices of provisions."[17] The discontent of the people caused local authorities to ask that outdoor relief be restored, and the extension of the workhouse system in the northern counties was opposed by violence.[18] Although the movement for universal suffrage known as Chartism began separately from the opposition to the Poor Law, and was even furthered to help the Liberal government as a diversion from anti-Poor-Law agitation,[19] by 1838 the Chartists' demands included "the total and unqualified repeal of the infamous New Poor Law Act, and a restoration of the spirit of the 43rd of Elizabeth, with such improvements as the circumstances of the country require."[20]

In a sense, therefore, although in their opposition to the New Poor Law the Chartists had the support of many conservatives,[21] the Chartist movement may be considered the rebellion that Hazlitt thought would follow the adoption of Malthus's plan. The old "poor laws [were not] again re-

---

15 Halévy, *A History of the English People, 1830-1841*, pp. 292-93. Cf. Nicholls, *op. cit.*, II, 356-65.

16 Nicholls, *op. cit.*, II, 360-61.

17 Fifth Report of the Poor Law Commissioners, p. 12, quoted in Nicholls, *op. cit.*, II, 363-64.

18 Halévy, *A History of the English People, 1830-1841*, pp. 293-94, 320, n.

19 *Ibid.*, pp. 299, 303-04.

20 *Northern Star*, July 21, 1838, quoted in Julius West, *A History of the Chartist Movement* (London: Constable and Co., 1920), p. 89. Cf. Halévy, *A History of the English People, 1830-1841*, pp. 304-05; and West, *op. cit.*, pp. 71, 95, 99, 100, 125, and 264.

21 Halévy, *A History of the English People, 1830-1841*, pp. 294-95; West, *op. cit.*, p. 129.

newed,"[22] but some concessions were made, if not in the principle, at least in the administration of the new law. The powers of the commission were renewed for only one year instead of three; the introduction of the workhouse system was further delayed in Lancashire and Yorkshire; and in several towns where the new workhouses were not large enough for all the paupers, the poor were employed on roads or some other public project and paid by voluntary subscriptions.[23] Although "indoor relief did not become universal, or even general,"[24] the triumph of the Chartists and Tories over the Whig government was in other respects short-lived. The Chartists had made preparations to gain their demands by force if their petition was refused, but in the summer of 1839, after serious riots had occurred in Birmingham and the government had made numerous arrests, the movement subsided for a time.[25] The Poor Law Commission was again renewed for only one year in 1840 and in 1841, thereby "weakening its influence" and encouraging opposition; but "in July 1842 . . . the commission was continued for another five years by *The 5th and 6th Victoria, cap.* 57, which for that time, at least, relieved the commissioners from the doubts and probabilities of a sudden termination of their functions, and gave confidence to their subordinates, and a certain reliance on the part of the union executives and the public."[26] If, however, the "rebellion" was less violent and less successful than pictured in Hazlitt's *Reply*, it must be remembered that the application of Malthus's principles had been considerably tempered.

---

[22] *Reply*, pp. 359-60.

[23] Halévy, *A History of the English People, 1830-1841*, pp. 323-24; Nicholls, *op. cit.*, II, 363.

[24] J. H. Clapham, "Work and Wages," *Early Victorian England, 1830-1865*, ed. G. M. Young (London: Oxford University Press, 1934), p. 34.

[25] Halévy, *A History of the English People, 1830-1841*, pp. 324-26, 332-35.

[26] Nicholls, *op. cit.*, II, 363.

CHAPTER VII

MALTHUS ON INSTITUTIONS

The causes to which Hazlitt attributes an artificially limited food supply are, for the most part, acknowledged by Malthus to have the effect pointed out in the *Reply*. Malthus does not, of course, share Hazlitt's condemnation of private property as a factor limiting subsistence; but Hazlitt, arguing that not even property is a necessary obstacle to "practical equality," is willing, in his criticism of the *Essay* as a practical work, to assume that this institution will continue, and sets out to show that, given private property and marriage, Malthus's proposals are not adequate to achieving the highest level of living consistent with human nature, natural resources, and these institutions.

Malthus agrees with Hazlitt and other critics that more land could be cultivated and that food wasted by the rich could be marketed for consumption by the poor;[1] and as a means to extending cultivation and raising the level of living, he puts much the same evaluation on "freedom" as found among the replies. ". . . The specific evil of taxation," Malthus frequently points out, "consists in the check which it gives to production . . . ."[2]

Industry cannot exist without foresight and security . . . . The poor Egyptian or Abyssinian farmer, without capital, who rents land, which is let out yearly to the highest bidder, and who is constantly subject to the demands of his tyrannical masters, to the casual plunder of an enemy, and, not unfrequently, to the violation of his miserable contract, can have no heart to be industrious, and if he had, could not exercise that industry with success.[3]

Not only industry, Malthus believes, but also the prudential check necessary to a high level of living depends upon "freedom."

---

1 *Essay* (2d ed.), Bk. III, chap. xi, pp. 477-78.
2 *Essay* (5th ed.), Vol. II, Bk. III, chap. vii, p. 361.
3 *Ibid.*, Bk. III, chap. xi, p. 475. Quoted in *Reply*, p. 259. Cf. *Essay* (2d ed.), Bk. I, chap. viii, pp. 109-16.

Ignorance and despotism seem to have no tendency to destroy the passion which prompts to increase; but they effectually destroy the checks to it from reason and foresight. . . . The miserable peasant who, from his political situation, feels little security of reaping what he has sown, will seldom be deterred from gratifying his passions by the prospect of inconveniences, which cannot be expected to press on him under three or four years.[4]

The freedom necessary to the industry and prudence of the poor in England, Malthus further acknowledges, is curtailed not only by the Poor Laws but by "the facility of combination among the rich, and its difficulty among the poor . . . ." This "want of freedom in the market of labour . . . operates to prevent the price of labour from rising at the natural period, and keeps it down some time longer; perhaps, till a year of scarcity, when the clamour is too loud, and the necessity too apparent to be resisted."[5]

These admissions, according to Hazlitt, make it absurd for Malthus to find no other method of dealing with poverty than the repeal of the Poor Laws. "If . . . nothing superfluous [were] now consumed by the higher classes," Malthus argues, if "no horses were used for pleasure, and no land . . . left uncultivated, a striking difference would appear in the state of actual population; but probably none whatever, in the state of the lower classes of people, with respect to the price of labour, and the facility of supporting a family."[6] But even if the improvement resulting from increased production or more generous distribution were, as Malthus says, only "for a time,"[7] it should not, Hazlitt argues, be sacrificed on that account;[8] and, elsewhere in the Reply, he suggests that the higher level of living attained would not be temporary but would resist downward pressure because greater prudence would be correlative with the increased utilization of resources or more equitable distribution.[9] Inferring from Malthus's

---

[4] Essay (5th ed.), Vol. II, Bk. III, chap. xi, pp. 474-75. Quoted in Reply, pp. 258-59.
[5] First Essay, p. 35. Quoted in Reply, p. 364.
[6] Essay (2d ed.), Bk. III, chap. xi, p. 478. Quoted in Reply, p. 364.
[7] Ibid., p. 478. Quoted in Reply, p. 347.
[8]. Reply, p. 348.
[9] Ibid., pp. 223, 228, 258-59, and passim.

ratios, his Poor-Law proposal, or his opposition to community ownership that Malthus deprecates populousness,[10] Hazlitt calls it absurd to fear an increase in population when, since the factors making for population growth also make the prudential check more effectual, poverty would not be any greater, at least, as numbers increased. If "during [the] progress of cultivation, the distress for want of food" would be no greater in proportion to the total population than it is at present, Malthus should realize that "the actual increase in population is to be considered so much clear gain, as so much addition to the sum of human happiness"[11]—unless, of course, he chooses to believe that "life is an evil, and whatever tends to promote it is an evil, [in which] case it would be well if all the inhabitants of the earth were to die some easy death to-morrow!"[12]

Mr. Malthus in different parts of his work [Hazlitt grants] makes a great *rout* about the distinction between *actual* and *relative* population, and lays it down that an actual increase of population is an advantage, except when it exceeds the means of subsistence; yet he here[13] seems to treat the proportion between the increase of population, and food, which he says has always continued pretty much the same, as the only thing to be attended to, and to represent the progressive increase of actual population, unless we could at the same time banish poverty entirely from the world, as a matter of the most perfect indifference, or rather the most dangerous experiment, that could be tried. Is not this being wilfully blind to the consequences of his own reasoning?[14]

---

10 The passage in the *Essay* that, Hazlitt finds, fairly "blocks up the road" to improvement is the one in which Malthus, after expressing his "astonishment, that all writers on the perfectibility of man and of society" did not foresee any danger from overpopulation "till the whole earth had been cultivated like a garden," goes on to say, "At every period during the progress of cultivation, from the present moment, to the time when the whole earth was become like a garden, the *distress for want of food would be constantly pressing on all mankind,* if they were equal. Though the produce of the earth might be increasing every year, population *would be increasing much faster;* and the redundancy must *necessarily* be repressed by the periodical or constant action of [vice and misery]." (*First Essay,* pp. 143-44. Quoted in *Reply,* p. 208. Hazlitt's italics.)

11 "Mr. Malthus has chosen to answer [the] question [whether we are to look upon an addition to the inhabitants of a state, if there is enough to support them, as a good or an evil] under the head, *modern philosophy,* so that he is secure of the protection of the court. I have been willing not to deprive him of this advantage, and have answered it under the same head." (*Reply,* p. 213.)

12 *Reply,* pp. 208-10.

13 *First Essay,* pp. 143-44. Quoted *supra,* n. 10.

14 *Reply,* p. 210.

Malthus's "own reasoning" seems to be that, as shown by a comparison of populous with thinly populated countries, the causes of populousness also diminish poverty. But Malthus, Hazlitt argues, although recognizing the effect of freedom on both industry and prudence and therefore on the production of food and the condition of the people, will not apply the lesson of Turkey, Abyssinia, and Egypt to benefit the English poor; and by denying "his own countrymen" the improvement he sees possible in foreign countries, involves " 'himself in absurdities and contradictions that would disgrace the lips of an ideot!' "[15]

The valid application of this argument is obscured by the misconceptions or misrepresentations of Malthus's position that are typical of controversy, especially with respect to (1) his attitude toward populousness and (2) the intended function of the Poor-Law plan. Other critics than Hazlitt, and disciples as well, infer that Malthus disapproves of increased population under any circumstances; and the critics reply that populousness, by making for a more efficient division of labor, ensuring cheap labor, creating new wants, and stimulating industry, provides an abundance for all.[16] Just as Hazlitt, after giving evidence that improved cultivation and increased population are good things "through inferior gradations," would "just reverse the reasoning of Mr. Malthus" and conclude that "they would continue so, proceeding upwards to the topmost round of the ladder, as far as population is concerned."[17] Ensor, Ingram, and Gray challenge Malthus to show how "it happen[s] that the same people grow rich as they grow more populous, and live better as they increase in numbers."[18]

To argue in this manner, Malthus replies, is to mistake "an effect for a cause," that is, to conclude "that . . . population was the cause of . . . prosperity, instead of . . . prosperity

---

[15] *Ibid.,* p. 259. Quotation "unidentified." (Notes to the *Reply,* p. 381.)

[16] Anderson, *op. cit.,* p. 41; Jarrold, *op. cit.,* pp. 28, 312-13; [Weyland], *A Short Inquiry,* p. 37; Ingram, *op. cit.,* pp. 18-19, 27-30; [Gray], *The Happiness of States,* p. 439; *Gray versus Malthus,* pp. 169, 174-76, 209; Grahame, *op. cit.,* pp. 112, 117, 275-77.

[17] *Reply,* p. 226.

[18] Ensor, *op. cit.,* p. 98. Cf. Ingram, *op. cit.,* pp. 18-19, 27; and *Gray versus Malthus,* p. 169.

being the cause of . . . population. . . ."[19] Malthus does not
consider the size or even the increase of population itself as
either a good or a bad sign. In examining the ratios we have
seen that he does not intend the geometrical ratio to stand for
an actual increase in population and that extending cultivation
seemed a "dangerous experiment" to some of Malthus's
disciples rather than to Malthus himself. "Scarcity and extreme poverty . . . may, or may not," he writes, "accompany
an increasing population,"[20] depending on whether it is effected
by an apparent or a real increase in wages and on the "preva-
lence of prudential habits, and a decided taste for the conveniences and comforts of life. . . ."[21] The low level of living
in thinly populated countries is to be attributed not to a small
population, but to the "tyranny" that discourages the prudential check and the production of food; and the high level of
living in more fully populated countries is attributable not to
populousness itself but to "freedom" from that tyranny. Malthus, therefore, does not disapprove of populousness per se
and does not have to accept either of Hazlitt's alternatives.
Hazlitt thinks of population being increased only by factors
that simultaneously encourage or at least do not discourage
the prudential check; and, like others among both critics and
disciples who interpret the *Essay* as opposed to any increase in
population, he neglects Malthus's repeated distinction between
desirable and undesirable means of encouraging population;
that is, between (1) granting freedom to individual enterprise within the limits of property and marriage and (2) methods, like charity or common ownership, that increase population without increasing food.[22]

With respect to the factors making for a higher or a lower
level of living, the accuracy of Hazlitt's charge of contradiction depends on whether Hazlitt believes that Malthus opposes
"freedom" for his own countrymen or whether he means only
that Malthus's proposal, if put into effect, would deny them
"freedom." The extent to which Hazlitt let himself under-

[19] *Essay* (2d ed.), Bk. III, chap. xi, p. 473.
[20] *Ibid.,* p. 472.
[21] *Essay* (5th ed.), Vol. III, Bk. III, chap. xiv, p. 34.
[22] *Essay* (2d ed.), Bk. III, chap. xi, pp. 470 ff.; Bk. IV, chap. iii, pp. 509-10.
Cf. *Essay* (5th ed.), Vol. III, Bk. III, chap. xiv, pp. 28-38.

stand Malthus's intention is perhaps disputable, although the indications are that he understood it better than, for purposes of detraction, he would acknowledge; at any rate, perhaps intentionally in order to destroy Malthus's influence, he fails to distinguish between Malthus's aims and the probable effects of the *Essay*—so that the denial of the rights of the poor that he thinks the *Essay* would cause becomes, in the *Reply,* equivalent to Malthus's *intention* to deny them their rights. Malthus, of course, makes no distinction between the kind or degree of freedom which he would allow the English farmer or laborer and that which he finds necessary to improvement in Turkey or Egypt or Abyssinia. What retards cultivation in these countries, he acknowledges, is the tyranny that, by making it impossible for the peasant to obtain an adequate return from his labor, robs him of the incentive and capital necessary to increased production; and it is freedom from this same kind of tyranny that Malthus champions for the English farmer. If he believes that the same degree of improvement would not result in England as would follow the establishment of such freedom in Turkey, Abyssinia, or Egypt, it is only because he considers agriculture in England to have already been encouraged by freedom until it has attained a more advanced state. Every government, Malthus believes, should "remove all obstacles, and give every facility, to the inclosure and cultivation of land; but when this has been done, the rest must be left to the operation of individual interest . . . ," and if the condition of the country is such that extending cultivation to new lands would require capital to be employed less profitably than "on the improvement of land already in cultivation," the farmer, if allowed to choose, will employ it on the latter.[23] The extent to which that freedom should be granted becomes, of course, a problem for further dispute. Hazlitt is not much worried about freedom of the capitalist; but other critics, like Ensor and Weyland, might have argued that in favoring taxes on imports and opposing the equalization of poor rates, Malthus was, in effect, denying the English farmer the freedom that was also denied peasants in Turkey, Egypt, and Abyssinia.

---

23 *Essay* (2d ed.), Bk. III, chap. xi, p. 479.

Similarly, with regard to the English laborer, Malthus favors the "freedom" that, by offering incentives to work hard and limit one's family, would make for the greatest relative subsistence. He does not condone the tyranny of combination among the employers any more than that of the Poor Laws. In his first edition he deprecates both as robbing the poor of "freedom in the market of labour," and designates combinations as "an unjust conspiracy" of the rich.[24] The freedom of the laborer, Malthus believes, must of course be within the restrictions imposed by private property; and if Hazlitt condemned private property as preventing more equitable distribution, he could say that Malthus, therefore, denies the English laborer any improvement—although, since Malthus consistently defends private property, it would still not be the kind of improvement he would grant the Turks and other oppressed peoples. Hazlitt, however, "meddle[s]" with the possibility of common ownership only as an "idle speculation." "Practical equality," he thinks, would be assured if the laborers were not prevented by the power of the employers and by the Combination Laws from bargaining for a wage commensurate with their labor; and it is Malthus's failure to propose an adequate means for granting them freedom of bargaining that makes Hazlitt condemn the *Essay* as a practical work.

Although acknowledging "the want of freedom in the market of labour" resulting from "the facility of combination among the rich," Malthus, as Hazlitt points out, relies for improvement on teaching the poor that they are responsible for their own poverty. The passage in the first *Essay* condemning combinations among the rich is quoted in the *Reply*, but only to show that Malthus "contradicts" himself in acknowledging *two* causes of low wages and then, to enforce his case against the Poor Laws, tracing unrest to the "ignorance" among "labouring men, during the late scarcities" that blamed "the evils of scarcity" and "the farmers and corn dealers . . . ."[25] Malthus argues that the establishment of "a government really free" depends upon the removal of this ignorance.[26] He

---

[24] *First Essay*, pp. 35-36.
[25] *Essay* (2d ed.), Bk. IV, chap. iv, pp. 553, 554, and 554, n. Quoted in *Reply*, pp. 363-64.
[26] *Ibid.*, p. 554.

regrets the recent encroachments on the liberty of the English people and the use of "organized force" to suppress disturbances, but the latter was necessary, he adds, to prevent "the most dreadful outrages . . . ."[27] But if, through the withdrawal of relief, it becomes clear to the poor how it lies within *their* power, and no one else's, to improve their condition, they would no longer threaten the proprietors; and the government, once the fear of revolution had passed, would repeal the tyrannous measures. Hazlitt, on the contrary, believes that as long as the proprietors have the power to depress wages at will and are selfishly determined to seek their own advantage at the expense of the poor, the repeal of the Poor Laws would not be enough to give the poor freedom in the labor market and enable them to demand a wage commensurate with their labor or, while the level of living is kept low by the power of the employers, enough to encourage the prudential check. Under these conditions, therefore, the denial of relief would only depress the poor still further and lead to revolution. Thus, although Malthus's *intention* is clearly not to deny the poor any possible advantage but to establish the freedom necessary to improvement, in terms of what Hazlitt considered the probable effects of the *Essay* and its proposals, Malthus is nevertheless denying the English laborer the improvement that he deems possible in Turkey, Egypt, or Abyssinia.

---

27 *Ibid.*, chap. vi, p. 526. Quoted in *Reply*, p. 349.

CHAPTER VIII

MORAL RESTRAINT AND THE
LEVEL OF LIVING

Like Hazlitt, most of the critics in the early period of the controversy think to refute Malthus's statement of population pressure by tracing vice and misery to other causes and citing the effects of human agencies in the production and distribution of food. Hazlitt's distinction between "freedom" and "tyranny" may be found in most of the replies, with institutions supposed to be unfavorable to greater production or more equitable distribution designated as "tyrannous" or inimical to the "free" exercise of some right. But Malthus acknowledges "immediate" checks "independent of . . . scarcity"[1] and argues for the unimpeded effects of those institutions which he thinks will make for the greatest relative subsistence —by encouraging both industry and the prudential check. The critics, therefore, in presenting evidence that the food supply varies and that different checks operate according to different political or moral influences, are not pointing out phenomena with which Malthus was unacquainted; and Malthus's designation of subsistence as the "ultimate" and "necessary" check to population is not refuted by these arguments.

On the other hand, if a critic goes further and takes issue with Malthus on the effect of a particular institution or shows that Malthus has minimized the effect of certain agencies on production or distribution or on the prudential check, he may have a case against Malthus's application of his principle if not against the principle itself. More than one critic, therefore, suggests the inadequacy of Malthus's plan to withdraw relief and, except for a program of education, leave the alleviation of poverty to the poor themselves. Hazlitt, more effectively than most of the critics, takes advantage of what, in view of the rising level of living in England in the nineteenth century, seems to have been the vulnerable point in Malthus's defense of his plan: that is, his argument that making greater amounts

---

[1] *Essay* (3d ed.), Vol. I, Bk. I, chap. ii, p. 15.

of food available would only increase population without raising the level of living. Other critics, although taking pains to show how more food could have been produced or distributed, give less attention to the question of relative production and distribution, or attribute greater relative subsistence to such physiological changes as decreased fecundity; whereas Hazlitt, in analyzing the factors that affect the prudential check, not only forecasts the higher level of living observable later in the century but also offers the explanation of it that appears in modern adaptations of Malthus's doctrine.

HAZLITT'S ANTICIPATION OF PLACE AND MILL

In modern books on population the higher level of living is usually explained by the fact of a differential birth rate, the inference that it results from voluntary restraint on the higher economic levels, and the further inference that (1) the conditions making for a higher level of living or (2) simply the attainment of that level enforces the prudential check. The differential birth rate is noted by both Malthus and his critics, but varying inferences are drawn to explain it and its relation to a greater command of goods. Some critics, although recognizing that a higher level of living makes for prudence, attack "moral restraint" as "immoral" in that it leads to promiscuity, violates God's decree to be fruitful and multiply, or retards the growth of population upon which a higher level of living depends.[2] Some attribute the lower birth rate in certain groups to the variation in "fecundity" accompanying social and economic change, and argue that the simultaneous increase of numbers and subsistence will not, therefore, lead to overpopulation.[3]

Malthus, of course, traces differential increase to voluntary restraint, but although he recognizes this restraint as at least

---

[2] Jarrold, op. cit., pp. 54-56; Gray versus Malthus, pp. 162-65, 291-98, 382, 425; [Weyland], A Short Inquiry, pp. 35-36; Weyland, Principles of Population and Production, pp. 165-66 and passim; Ingram, op. cit., pp. 4-5, 30-40, 74-75, 100 ff.; Grahame, op. cit., pp. 166-69, 198-99, 234-45, 272-73; Ensor, op. cit., pp. 181, 195-96, 498.

[3] Jarrold, op. cit., pp. 261-64, 268-73, 288; [Gray], The Happiness of States, pp. 353, 447, 450-55, 461-62; Gray versus Malthus, pp. 122-24, 129-31, 146-48, 156-57, 283-89; Weyland, Principles of Population and Production, pp. 62-83, 107-08.

partly responsible for the difference between the Englishman's and the Abyssinian's standard of living, he does not believe that volition, even if the Poor Laws were repealed, could effect a very great improvement in the condition of the poor in England.[4] Similarly in the first edition, he depreciates the effect of combination on the condition of the poor. "But though the rich by unfair combinations, contribute frequently to prolong a season of distress among the poor; yet no possible form of society could prevent the almost constant action of misery, upon a great part of mankind, if in a state of inequality, and upon all, if all were equal."[5] He is not, we have noticed, involving himself in a contradiction here, for he at least wishes the English worker to be free to work where he pleases and demand a wage commensurate with his labor; but his conception of man as a "compound-being" prevents him from believing that any means of enforcing moral restraint could be effective to more than a very limited degree. Unwilling to resign themselves, however, to so limited a degree of improvement, Godwin, Coleridge, Southey, and Hazlitt point out the "fallacy" of insisting that people "will always be the same, whether circumstances are the same or not."[6] Like those believing in physiological checks, they argue that the birth rate may be affected by social and economic conditions, but they foresee voluntary rather than involuntary restraints maintaining a level of living once it has been reached. Having more faith in the power of circumstances to increase the command of reason over passion, these critics come closer than Malthus to predicting the higher level of living accompanying the subsequent increase in productive capacity, and also to explaining it as later writers have explained it.

This greater faith in reason links the radicals of the first period of the controversy with the "philosophical radicals" of the second and the classical expression given to the principle of population by John Stuart Mill. Hazlitt, especially, seems to anticipate the position of Francis Place and Mill. For one thing, the goal of these men is not common ownership but more

---

[4] *Essay* (2d ed.) Bk. IV, chap. iii, p. 504.
[5] *First Essay*, p. 36.
[6] *Reply*, pp. 286-87.

equitable distribution within the system of private property; whereas Hall and Godwin speak of effective checking only in a state of equality of property and, for any intermediate improvement, rely on increased productivity.[7] Coleridge and Southey, it is true, consider the prudential check as a means to "improvability," as distinguished from "the system of equality" and "perfectibility,"[8] but they do not specify the factors affecting the check or rendering its use effectual in raising the level of living.

Since the "philosophical radicals" are concerned, not with defending a state of equality, but with discovering means, consistent with the system of private property, for giving the poor an increased command of goods, the preventive check becomes more clearly a *means to improvement* rather than simply a *means of securing improvement.* The former, of course, is the function Malthus assigns to this check, but since Place and Mill find improvement more dependent on institutions than Malthus believes, they are more optimistic than Malthus that poverty can be diminished. Mill designates "Malthus's population principle" as "a banner, and points of union" among "the little group of young men who were the first propagators of what was afterwards called 'Philosophic Radicalism.' . . ."

This great doctrine, originally brought forward as an argument against the indefinite improvability of human affairs, we took up with ardent zeal in the contrary sense, as indicating the sole means of realizing that improvability by securing full employment at high wages to the whole labouring population through a voluntary restriction of the increase of their numbers.[9]

As a means to "voluntary restriction," however, physical means of preventing conception were suggested or at least condoned. John Stuart Mill, Field points out, "stands almost or quite alone" among his confreres "in the less radical position" of advocating "the observance by the married of what might

---

7 Hall, *The Effects of Civilization* (1st ed.), pp. 35-45, 217-19; Hall, *The Effects of Civilization* (2d ed.), Appendix, pp. 343-47; Godwin, *Thoughts,* pp. 72-73; Godwin, *Of Population,* pp. 309-10, 449, 469-72, 490, 497-98, 526-34, 560.

8 [Southey], "Malthus's Essay on Population," *op. cit.,* p. 296; Potter, *op. cit.,* pp. 1061-68.

9 John Stuart Mill, *Autobiography* (New York: Henry Holt and Company, n.d.), chap. iv, p. 105.

still be called moral restraint," but "even he doubtless had no
intention of excluding physical means of prevention."[10] James
Mill cautiously recommends contraception,[11] but "the first unequivocal advocacy of this form of check appears to have been
that contained in Francis Place's *Illustrations and Proofs of
the Principle of Population,* the introduction to which is dated
February 1, 1822."[12] In Professor Himes's words, Place tries
to reconcile the "false dichotomy in the Malthus-Godwin controversy"[13] by dividing the responsibility for poverty more
evenly between institutions and the poor themselves. ". . .
To better the condition of the working people," Place requires
"a repeal of (1) all the laws, relating to the combinations of
workmen to increase their wages," (2) "the laws restraining
Emigration," and (3) "all restrictive laws on trade, commerce
and manufacture, and particularly the corn laws";[14] but he
agrees with Malthus that " 'it is not in the nature of things,
that any permanent and general improvement in the condition
of the poor can be effected without an increase in the preventive check . . . .' "[15] From his own experience—including
incontinence before marriage at nineteen and, despite his poverty, fifteen children born afterward—Place realized the im-
practicability of moral restraint[16] and of Malthus's plan to
enforce it by "excluding children from parish aid . . . ."[17]
He urges, therefore, that physical means be used to prevent
conception.[18] Only in this way can morals be so improved that
"moral restraint" may become an effective check, for "the
great corrective (of promiscuity and other vices) must be
looked for in proportioning the labourers to the demand for
labour, and to the increase of the means of subsistence."[19] But
Place continues to rely on contraception as well, as a means for
obtaining and securing improvement. "There appears, upon a

---

[10] Field, *op. cit.,* pp. 45-46.
[11] *Ibid.,* pp. 46-47.
[12] *Ibid.,* p. 47.
[13] Place, *op. cit.,* Introduction, p. 38.
[14] *Ibid.,* pp. 171-72.
[15] *Ibid.,* p. 173. Quoted from *Essay* (5th ed.), Vol. III, Bk. IV, chap. xiii,
pp. 299-300.
[16] *Ibid.,* Introduction, p. 10.
[17] *Ibid.,* p. 173.
[18] *Ibid.,* pp. 173-74.
[19] *Ibid.,* p. 178.

view of the whole case, no just cause for despair, but much for hope, that moral restraint will increase, and that such physical means of prevention will be adopted, as prudence may point out and reason may sanction, and the supply of labour be thus constantly kept below the demand for labour, and the amount of population be always such as the means of comfortable subsistence can be provided for."[20]

Except that Place favors contraception and that Hazlitt, in combating Malthus's emphasis on the poor's responsibility, puts greater emphasis on the responsibility of institutions, this position is essentially Hazlitt's. If not prevented by oppressive institutions, Hazlitt believes, the poor can proportion their numbers to the available food, and the moral and economic levels will rise together, so that the higher the level of living, the more secure it is rendered by the prudential check. Contraception fits in with Hazlitt's or, rather, Malthus's system as simply another preventive check.[21] Although characterized by Malthus as vicious, it is "moral" enough from the point of view of later writers. With regard to the end in view and the faculties involved in its operation there is no difference from the "moral restraint" of Malthus or Hazlitt or Godwin. The use of contraceptives may require a lesser degree of control over passion—or perhaps render a certain degree of control more effectual in limiting births—but both "voluntary restriction" and "moral restraint" presuppose (1) the domination of reason over passion as the result of a calculation of consequences to the individual and (2) a resulting increase in the happiness of the greatest number.

Hazlitt's Anticipation of Modern Population Theory

Because of the rising level of living that followed the opening up of international trade during the nineteenth century, later writers can agree with Hazlitt that Malthus underestimates the effect of increased resources on the condition of the people. John Stuart Mill, who substitutes the "law of diminishing returns" for the arithmetical ratio in stating the principle of population, explains more fully than Malthus the

---

[20] *Ibid.,* pp. 178-79.
[21] Cf. Fairchild, *op. cit.,* pp. 141-42.

factors that may postpone the operation of this law and the effects of increased productivity on both population and the level of living. After a country has "passed beyond a rather early stage in the progress of agriculture," Mill points out, every increase in population "will always, unless there is a simultaneous improvement in production, diminish the share which on a fair division would fall to each individual. An increased production, in default of unoccupied tracts of fertile land, or of fresh improvements tending to cheapen commodities, can never be obtained but by increasing the labour in more than the same proportion."[22] The effect of "fresh improvements," however, were less evident in Malthus's day than in 1857, when "the great mechanical inventions of Watt, Arkwright, and their contemporaries" had tremendously increased "the return to labour" and "the extension of improved processes of agriculture" had made "even the land yield . . . a greater produce in proportion to the labour employed."[23] Malthus had not foreseen the "improvements" that would increase the return from agriculture or, by increasing the return for labor expended in manufacturing, would multiply the products that could be exchanged for food produced in newly exploited territories; nor had he expected the development in transportation which, in effect, extended the continent of Europe far beyond the limits Malthus recognized. He was too ready, we know now, to think of the extension of cultivation only as the utilization of inferior lands, the return from which would not be proportionate to the additional labor and capital expended on them. He seems to have considered improvements of land largely in terms of fertilizing, and objects that, as pasture land is turned into farm land, manure would become increasingly difficult to obtain.[24] Moreover, he minimized not only the possibility of exploiting natural resources more fully but also the effect of even "sudden cultivation" as "tend[ing] to improve [the] condition [of the poor] for [only] a time . . . ."[25] Mill, however, explains that "improvements" tending "to give

[22] John Stuart Mill, *Principles of Political Economy* (London: Longmans, Green and Co., 1923), Bk. I, chap. xiii, p. 190.
[23] *Ibid.*, p. 193.
[24] Essay (2d ed.), Bk. III, chap. ii, p. 371. Cf. chap. xi, pp. 478-82.
[25] *Essay* (2d ed.), Bk. III, chap. xi, p. 478.

new motives or new facilities to production" may be so great
as to maintain a higher level of living as well as encourage
population.

After a degree of density has been obtained, sufficient to allow the
principal benefits of a combination of labour, all further increase tends in
itself to mischief, so far as regards the average condition of the people;
but the progress of improvement has a counteracting operation, and allows
of increased numbers without any deterioration, and even consistently
with a higher average of comfort.[26]

Mill's explanation of the higher level of living, moreover,
is essentially the one we have found in the *Reply*. Hazlitt, like
Malthus and unlike some of the other critics, does not believe
that the level of living can be raised by keeping production
ahead of the potential increase of population, but, unlike Malthus, he thinks that the prudential check—rendered more responsive to changing conditions—would keep the increased
population from monopolizing, even in the long run, the effects
of increased purchasing power.

. . . Though improvement [Mill agrees] may during a certain space of
time keep up with, or even surpass, the actual increase of population, it
assuredly never comes up to the rate of increase of which population is
capable; and nothing could have prevented a general deterioration in the
condition of the human race, were it not that population has in fact been
restrained. Had it been restrained still more, and the same improvements
taken place, there would have been a larger dividend than there now is,
for the nation or the species at large.[27]

Mill agrees also that there is a "habitual standard . . . down
to which [the labouring classes] will multiply, but not lower,"
and that factors making for increased production elevate this
standard, or, in Hazlitt's terms, render the prudential check
responsive to the fear of less vice and misery. For, in defining
"improvement," Mill includes "improvements in institutions,
education, opinions, and human affairs" as tending to give
"new motives or new facilities to production,"[28] and here he
adds that "every advance . . . in education, civilization, and

---

[26] *Op. cit.*, pp. 191-93.
[27] *Ibid.*, p. 193.
[28] *Ibid.*, p. 192.

social improvement, tends to raise th[e] standard" of comfort which the people will not sacrifice for larger families.[29] Looking back upon the period of expansion, then, Mill explains it much as Hazlitt did in anticipation.

. . . There is no doubt that [this standard] is gradually, though slowly, rising in the more advanced countries of Western Europe. Subsistence and employment have never increased more rapidly than in the last forty years [*ca.* 1822—*ca.* 1862], but every census since 1821 showed a smaller proportional increase of population than that of the period preceding . . . .[30]

Mill's explanation of the relation between population and the level of living is substantially that of modern writers on population who have interpreted more recent population phenomena in terms of Malthus's principle, although there are, of course, modern theories that reject, at least in part, the Malthusian explanation of population growth and decline. Catholic writers reject even the modern modification of Malthus's theory as not proved or as incapable of proof, and recognize "no problem either theoretical or practical" with regard to population pressure.

The[ir] usual statement runs to the effect that with an efficient organization of industry and an equitable distribution of wealth, among a frugal and industrious people who place no limit on the physiological power to reproduce after marriage, there would never be any undue pressure of population on subsistence except locally and temporarily, provided a considerable number of the population lived a life of religious celibacy, others deferred marriage to a late age, and others emigrated when the region became congested.[31]

Another doctrine, reminiscent of Jarrold, Gray, and especially Weyland, is "that the power to conceive and procreate children is subject to cyclical variations of centuries in length . . . . The fall in the European birth rate in the past half century is said to be due [, therefore,] to the entrance of the race on one of the cyclical periods of decline in human fer-

29 *Ibid.,* p. 161.
30 *Ibid.*
31 Reuter, *op. cit.,* p. 172.

tility."[32]   This theory, however, is not generally accepted. Professor Reuter dismisses Corrado Gini's version of it as "ignoring or denying the existence of facts not in harmony with the prepossessions";[33] and Professor Fairchild agrees that the lower birth rate since 1870 has been probably due, not to a "decline in biological fertility" but to "a decline in the frequency of mating, or steps . . . taken by married couples to prevent mating from resulting in pregnancies."[34] According to Carle C. Zimmerman the decline in population attributed by some writers to biological factors and by the Malthusians to economic ones can be traced, in part, to "non-material factors in the general standard of living." The kind of family life, apart from the family's command of goods, affects the birth rate; and the "antagonisms in the race for material goods [that] arise among the social classes and among the various nationalist groups when such goods become the primary objective in any civilization" discourage the increase of even material well-being and consequently of population.[35] But Professor Zimmerman makes this criticism not so much to dispute as to limit the "validity [of the Malthusian doctrine] in the field of standards of living. . . ."[36]

The relationship explained by Mill as existing among land, population, improvements in production, and level of living has been expressed by later writers in various formulas, of which the following are typical:

(1) Plane of living $= \dfrac{\text{income}}{\text{population}}$

Income $= \dfrac{\text{natural resources x industrial}}{\text{technique x labor power}}$[37]

---

[32] *Ibid.*, p. 173. Cf. Corrado Gini, "The Cyclical Rise and Fall of Population," *Population Lectures on the Harris Foundation, 1929* (Chicago: University of Chicago Press, 1930).

[33] *Op. cit.*, pp. 174-75.

[34] *Op. cit.*, pp. 138-39.

[35] Carle C. Zimmerman, *Consumption and Standards of Living* (New York: D. Van Nostrand Company, 1936), pp. 212-13.

[36] *Ibid.*, p. 214.

[37] *Ibid.*, p. 205. As Zimmerman adds, "these formulas, although stated in terms of mathematical relations, have, of course, no precise significance. They are merely forms to balance a number of factors which theoretically contribute to one side or the other."

$$(2) \quad \text{Level of living} = \frac{\text{land x economic culture}^{38}}{\text{population}}$$

Professor Fairchild defines "economic culture" as "the whole combination of human devices and instruments of every sort whereby man is able to increase the volume and variety of the things he needs and wishes beyond what nature would offer by herself."[39] The application of labor, then, is implied in this term rather than separately expressed. The population best qualified in size to achieve the maximum per capita return from a given combination of "land" and "economic culture" or "natural resources" and "industrial technique" is generally known as the "optimum." It is that population beyond which, in Mill's words, every increase in numbers will "diminish the share which on a fair division would fall to each individual," unless new resources be made available or the more complete exploitation of the old ones be made possible. According to Professor Thompson "this economic theory of the optimum is that there is a certain size of population which is best fitted to secure the maximum economic returns per head from a given body of natural resources under a given system of production, or perhaps better, under a given type of social and economic organization."[40]

What Malthus did not realize is, according to this theory, the possibility of changes in the "system of production" or in "social and economic organization" establishing a new and much greater optimum and the effect of that change on the level of living. Professor Thompson, after noting that population growth during the nineteenth century substantiates rather than invalidates Malthus's "chief contention" that population will increase with the means of subsistence, adds that what "Malthus did not clearly foresee, was that for a time, at least," the new power of production "would enable man not only to care for his almost unrestricted increase in numbers, but would

---

[38] Fairchild, *op. cit.*, p. 75.

[39] *Ibid.*, p. 63.

[40] *Op. cit.*, p. 393. The effect of "social and economic organization" is obvious, as Malthus pointed out in Egypt and Abyssinia, for "a magnificent endowment of natural resources and technology may be so clogged by an antiquated social economy that only a fraction of its potential benefit is realized." (Fairchild, *op. cit.*, p. 75.)

also enable this larger population to live better than ever before."[41] Malthus, we have seen, acknowledges that greater productivity might improve the condition of the people "for a time,"[42] but in thinking of this improvement as transient or according to Professor Thompson, as "issu[ing] in greater hardship,"[43] Malthus underestimates the effectiveness of the prudential check "in keeping man's numbers within bounds."[44] Professor Fairchild also attributes the higher level of living accompanying increased numbers to the operation of the prudential check. Although population may remain even greater than the new optimum, he points out, a higher level of living may be attained. Overpopulation—or the condition of having too many people relative to land and economic culture to allow the maximum standard of living—"has been the chronic and virtually universal state of human societies from time immemorial," for "as man's technology has improved," population has never been retarded enough "to allow him to apply the full benefit of his cultural achievements to improving his material situation." There has often, nevertheless, been "enough of a lag to allow some betterment of the level of living . . . ."[45]

Since an increase in population cannot immediately follow increased income, whereas "the improvement in the level of living can take place almost instantaneously if the material requirements are available," the level of living is more likely to get the immediate benefit of the increased availability of goods, and once a higher level of living is established it "resists downward pressure very stubbornly." If the increase in income, then, is rapid enough to let the level of living get ahead of population increase, the former can hold its own when it must be weighed against marriage or children.[46] Thus, about 1870, when "the growth of population . . . beg[a]n to catch up with the expansion of land and economic culture and could not continue without a sacrifice of the level of living," it was

---

41 *Op. cit.*, p. 45. Cf. Fairchild, *op. cit.*, pp. 135-36.
42 *Essay* (2d ed.), Bk. III, chap. xi, p. 478.
43 Cf. *Essay* (5th ed.), Bk. III, chap. iv, pp. 304-05.
44 Thompson, *op. cit.*, p. 45.
45 *Op. cit.*, p. 89.
46 *Ibid.*, pp. 131-32.

probably the preventive check rather than any decrease in fertility that caused the birth rate to decline.[47]

These writers, therefore, in their interpretation of the increasing numbers and the rising level of living in the nineteenth century, and the declining birth rate since 1870, would agree with Hazlitt that, although these phenomena do not invalidate Malthus's principle, they show the incompleteness of the *Essay* as a practical work. While insisting that nothing could be done to improve the condition of the poor except by withdrawing relief, Malthus depreciates "sudden cultivation" as likely to improve the condition of the poor for only a time,[48] and although he believes that agriculture should be encouraged by facilitating enclosure and taxing imports, that taxes on land should be kept as low as possible, and that employers should not combine to keep wages low, he represents the effects of these measures, as applied to the England of his time, as insignificant compared with the results of withdrawing poor relief. It is outside the scope of this paper to analyze the factors that, accompanying improvements in technology and transportation, allowed the English people to enjoy the equivalent of "sudden cultivation." Enclosures, defended by Malthus, probably helped, but so did the modification and finally, in 1846, the repeal of the Corn Laws. Lower taxes, advocated by both Malthus and Hazlitt, seem to have had a share in raising the real wages of the poor; and the increased mobility of labor, mine and factory legislation, and Grahame's "natural" remedy of emigration, must all be taken into consideration.[49] The influence of trade unions at this time is less obvious.

---

[47] *Ibid.*, p. 138. Cf. Reuter, *op. cit.*, pp. 174-75. The tendency of a level of living to resist downward pressure also explains the improved conditions among those who remain after "a sudden and extensive migratory movement . . . . If the relief is immediate and widespread it will be followed by a rise in wages or by a fall in prices. In either case, there is a rise in the standard of living . . . . Once they become accustomed to this somewhat higher standard of living, they will make every effort to maintain it. In order to maintain the higher standard, they may exercise control over the forces of reproduction, and the marriage and birth rates may decline. (Reuter, *op. cit.*, pp. 213-14. Cf. Fairchild, *op. cit.*, pp. 231-38.)

[48] *Essay* (2d ed.), Bk. III, chap. xi, p. 478.

[49] J. H. Clapham, "Work and Wages," *Early Victorian England, 1830-1865,* pp. 3-76; Trevelyan, *op. cit.*, pp. 267-80.

Probably, however, as Friedrich Engels argued in the forties, they had sometimes helped to start "a more rapid rise of wages after a crisis" than the unstimulated working of economic law (or force) would have permitted, in a world in which the bargaining powers of employer and employed were often singularly unequal. Besides that, and vastly more important, they were bringing a new security, dignity, and self-confidence into the estate of the wage-earners; although it was still usual in other estates to view them with suspicion, or hostility, or uneasy contempt.[50]

Perhaps, then, although not increasing wages directly, the unions helped to raise the level of living, as Hazlitt suggested, by encouraging the prudential check. But more important in supporting Hazlitt's criticism of the *Essay* than an enumeration of the particular institutions contributing to improvement, is the fact that there *was* improvement and that it was effected by means that Malthus depreciated *in toto* in favor of cutting off relief. "By 1865 wages were, on the average, nearly 20 per cent above the level of 1848 . . . . The prices of necessaries had also risen, but certainly not so much."[51] Population increased rapidly but not rapidly enough to prevent a rise in real wages, and when it apparently became necessary to curtail population increase in order to maintain the level of living, the birth rate began to fall. The command of goods which people were not willing to sacrifice for marriage or children was, it seems, higher in 1870 than it had been thirty years before.

Thus what Hazlitt calls the "responsiveness" of the prudential check to changed conditions seems to have been increased, as he predicts, with increased population and productivity. ". . . As . . . increased population would be the consequence of greater industry and knowledge, it would, one should think, denote of itself, that the people would be less liable to unforeseen accidents, and less likely to involve themselves in wilful distress than before."[52] As Malthus shows, however, population may increase—at the expense of the level of living—without a corresponding increase in production; and according to Professor Fairchild, increased production alone

---

[50] Clapham, *op. cit.*, p. 61. The quotation is identified as being from Engel's *Condition of the Working Classes*, p. 145.

[51] Clapham, *op. cit.*, p. 76.

[52] *Reply*, p. 225.

is not enough to raise the level of living. "If there is a slow, gradual, continuous improvement, such as has been going on from time immemorial in economic culture, time is allowed for the slow processes of population to take effect, and most if not all the advantage goes to the population factor, leaving the level of living unchanged."[53] There are, moreover, the "non-material factors" accompanying increased productivity and a rising material level of living that tend "to inhibit the further development of wealth and material well-being."[54] But although we must qualify Hazlitt's inference that prudence and the level of living are functions of production and total population, the increased availability of food seems to have been more of a factor in improving the condition of the poor than Malthus allows for; and, as Hazlitt predicts,[55] an acquaintance "with comfort and decency" seems to have enforced the prudential check in order to maintain a level of living. Malthus, too, notes that the "habits of prudential restraint . . . most frequently arise from the custom of enjoying conveniences and comforts,"[56] but since he thinks of increased production mainly in terms of using inferior soils and since he is skeptical of any "great change" in the practice of moral restraint, he puts little faith in "sudden cultivation" and its effect upon the welfare of the poor.[57]

Conclusion

If, as history and later writers indicate, Malthus relied too exclusively on one means of improvement, the practical application of which met with questionable success, and depreciated the means through which the condition of the poor seems actually to have been improved, most of the early critics can be credited with suggesting the inadequacy of the *Essay* as a practical work. In the first place, regardless of their politics, all the critics that we have examined believed that the withdrawal of relief would either immediately make the poor still more wretched or, by discouraging agriculture and commerce,

---

53 *Op. cit.,* p. 132.
54 Zimmerman, *op. cit.,* p. 212.
55 *Reply,* p. 312. Cf. pp. 258, 308, 314, and *passim.*
56 *Essay* (5th ed.), Vol. II, Bk. III, chap. viii, p. 392.
57 *Essay* (2d ed.), Bk. III, chap. xi, p. 478.

cause eventual scarcity. In the second place, as an alternative to checking population by withdrawing poor relief, and especially as a denial that food can increase only arithmetically and that, therefore, vice and misery must be forced upon the poor in order to keep down their numbers, the critics urged that more food be made available by increasing production or equalizing distribution, and to these ends proposed various means that we have already examined.

But if Malthus depended too exclusively on enforcing the prudential check, he also seems to have underestimated the effectiveness of this check in maintaining a level of living; and those critics approach still closer to the weakness of Malthus's proposals who go beyond pointing out the possibility of greater production or more equitable distribution and argue that this improvement would be secured because the control of the sexual passion is not constant but increases with the conditions that make it more desirable. Thus, those critics who undertake to defend "perfectibility" or an approach to it, are forced into a favorable position for attacking the practicality of the *Essay* and are supplied, through the perfectionist psychology of Godwin or some variant like Hazlitt's with the argument for supporting their criticism.

Hazlitt's opposition to the *Essay,* we have seen, may be accounted for by his "revolutionary philosophy" as both modified and supported by his explanation of human behavior. Because it seemed likely to disproportion still further the suffering that was already too unequally divided between the rich and the poor, Hazlitt attacks Malthus's Poor-Law proposal, explaining that as long as the rich selfishly abuse the power of property and until "habit and circumstance" make the poor more prudent, trying to force a calculation of consequences among the poor will not improve their condition. He turns, then, to ridiculing the *Essay* in order to destroy its influence, and finds it vulnerable in its attack on *Political Justice.* Although repudiating "perfectibility" himself, he argues that it is absurd to say that a perfect society would be destroyed because of imperfections that would have prevented its realization, for men whose calculation of consequences could establish a perfect society could also prevent overpopulation.

However, Hazlitt sees more in this argument than an objection to Malthus's logic, for he believes that man is psychologically capable of *approaching* perfection and that the increased control of passion will be correlative with that approach and the decrease of poverty accompanying it. Thus, when he mistakes, or chooses to mistake, Malthus's warning against equality as a warning against increased cultivation, he argues that the "freedom" making for increased cultivation would also make for increased moral restraint; and when he defends a state of at least "practical equality," he argues that if the laborers were "free" to bargain for a higher wage, the increased acquaintance with "comfort and decency" and the assurance of a reward commensurate with the sacrifice required, would do more than poverty to enforce industry and the prudential check.

Hazlitt's opposition to the *Essay,* therefore, and his defense of equality, assumes very much the pattern of Godwin's. Disinterestedness or benevolence, subordinated by Malthus to self-love, becomes again a factor in improvement. Reason, depreciated in the *Essay,* collaborates with the proper affections to control desire. Nature, held responsible by Malthus for the great mass of evil, surrenders 'her burden once more to institutions. The psychology is different from Godwin's, in that the "perfect" man does not figure in Hazlitt's predictions, and Godwin's "perfect" society is curtailed to a "practical equality" with marriage and private property, but this practical equality must be fostered by benevolence, maintained by mastery over passion, and freed from the institutions that artificially limit the production and distribution of goods and confirm selfish or irrational behavior.

But the differences from Godwin are important also. Godwin points out how prudence increases with the factors making it desirable and infers, therefore, that the prudential check would prevent overpopulation in a state of equality, but he limits the application of this argument to such a state. In *Of Population,* not wishing to "disput[e] about the most eligible form of human society,"[58] he suggests, like Anderson and Gardner, only more extensive and intensive cultivation. Haz-

---

[58] *Of Population,* p. 469.

litt, however, by applying this argument to an intermediate state of "practical equality" goes further toward predicting the rising level of living, the declining birth rate, and adaptation of Malthus's theory by Place and Mill and modern writers on population.

Since Hazlitt's day the working classes have gained both politically and economically. Specific measures advocated by Hazlitt, others suggested by his opponents, and still other influences unforeseen by either, have played a part in this improvement, but so many and so varied are these factors that it would be a presumptuous scholar indeed who weighed the respective contributions of "reason" or "self-love" or "benevolence." After more than a century, "nature" still has a way of "limiting improvement" and has come to employ forms of "vice and misery" that would have horrified Malthus, who although he dispassionately catalogued forms of suffering throughout the world was really a kindhearted man. There is evidence, of which we need feel no less sure because it cannot be presented scientifically, that self-love has played a considerable part in applying these checks. But it can hardly be said that, in eliminating them or softening them, the possibilities of reason and benevolence have ever been exhausted.

BIBLIOGRAPHY

Writings by William Hazlitt

Hazlitt, William. *The Complete Works of William Hazlitt.* Edited by P. P. Howe. Vols. I, VII, XI, XVII, and XIX. London: J. M. Dent and Sons, Ltd., 1930-34.

Other Primary Sources

Books and Pamphlets

Anderson, James. *A Calm Investigation of the Circumstances that Have Led to the Present Scarcity of Grain in Britain.* . . . 2d ed. London: John Cumming, 1801.

Bentham, Jeremy. *Observations on the Poor Bill.* London: William Clowes and Sons, 1838.

Brydges, Sir Egerton. *The Population and Riches of Nations.* . . . Paris: J. J. Paschoud; London: Rob. Triphook, 1819.

Burke, Edmund. *The Works of Edmund Burke.* Vol. V. Boston: Little, Brown and Company, 1866.

Crabbe, George. *The Village.* In *A Collection of English Poems, 1660-1800.* Edited by R. S. Crane. New York: Harper and Bros., 1932.

Darwin, Erasmus. *The Temple of Nature.* London: J. Johnson, 1803.

De Quincey, Thomas. *The Collected Writings of Thomas De Quincey.* Edited by David Masson. Vol. IX. London: A. & C. Black, 1897.

Eden, Sir Frederic Morton. *The State of the Poor. A History of the Labouring Classes in England, with Parochial Reports.* Abridged and edited by A. G. L. Rogers. London: George Routledge & Sons, 1928.

Ensor, George. *An Inquiry Concerning the Population of Nations.* . . . London: Effingham Wilson, 1818.

Gardner, Edward. *Reflections upon the Evil Effects of an Increasing Population, upon the High Price of Provisions.* . . . Glocester: R. Raikes, 1800.

Godwin, William. *An Enquiry Concerning Political Justice, and Its Influence on Morals and Happiness.* 2 vols. London: G. G. and J. Robinson, 1793.

————. *An Enquiry Concerning Political Justice, and Its Influence on Morals and Happiness.* 2d ed. corrected. 2 vols. London: G. G. and J. Robinson, 1796.

————. *Thoughts Occasioned by the Perusal of Dr. Parr's Spital Sermon* . . . *Being a Reply to the Attacks of Dr. Parr, Mr. Mack-*

intosh, the Author of the Essay on Population and Others. London: G. G. and J. Robinson, 1801.

————. *Of Population. An Enquiry Concerning the Power of Increase in the Numbers of Mankind.* London: Longman, Hurst, Rees, Orme, and Brown, 1820.

Grahame, James. *An Inquiry into the Principle of Population Including an Exposition of the Causes and the Advantages of a Tendency to Exuberance of Numbers in Society.* . . . Edinburgh: Archibald Constable and Co.; London: Longman, Hurst, Rees, Orme, and Brown, 1816.

[Gray, Simon, under pseudonym of] Purves, George. *Gray versus Malthus. The Principles of Population and Production Investigated.* . . . London: Longman, Hurst, Rees, Orme, and Brown, 1818.

Gray, S[imon]. *The Happiness of States; or, an Inquiry Concerning Population.* . . . [2d ed.] London: J. Hatchard and Son, and Longman and Company; Edinburgh: A. Constable and Co., and Waugh and Innes, 1819.

Hall, Charles. *The Effects of Civilization on the People in European States.* London: T. Ostell and C. Chappel, 1805.

————. *The Effects of Civilization on the People in European States, with an Appendix Containing Observations on the Principal Conclusion in Mr. Malthus's Essay on Population.* 2d ed. London: M. Jones, and Craddock and Co., 1813.

Hansard. *Parliamentary History.* Vols. XXXII (1795-96) and XXXIV (1800).

————. *Parliamentary Debates.* Vols. VIII (1807) and XXXIII (1816).

————. *Parliamentary Debates.* (3d series). Vol. XXV (1834).

Ingram, Robert Acklom. *Disquisitions on Population; in Which the Principles of the Essay on Population, by the Rev. T. R. Malthus, Are Examined and Refuted.* London: J. Hatchard, 1808.

Jarrold, T. *Dissertations on Man, Philosophical, Physiological, and Political; in Answer to Mr. Malthus's "Essay on the Principle of Population."* London: Cadell and Davis, and Burditt, 1806.

Malthus, Thomas Robert. *First Essay on Population, 1798.* London: Macmillan and Co., Ltd., 1926.

Malthus, T[homas] R[obert]. *An Essay on the Principle of Population; or, a View of Its Past and Present Effects on Human Happiness; with an Inquiry into Our Prospects Respecting the Future Removal or Mitigation of the Evils Which It Occasions.* [2d ed.] London: J. Johnson, 1803.

————. *An Essay on the Principle of Population.* . . . 3d ed. 2 vols. London: J. Johnson, 1806.

————. *An Essay on the Principle of Population.* . . . 5th ed. 3 vols. London: John Murray, 1817.

Mill, John Stuart. *Autobiography.* New York: Henry Holt and Company, n. d.

————. *Principles of Political Economy.* London: Longmans, Green and Co., 1923.

Napier, Macvey. *Selections from the Correspondence of the Late Macvey Napier.* Edited by Macvey Napier. London: Macmillan and Company, 1879.

Owen, Robert. *A New View of Society: or, Essays on the Formation of Human Character Prefatory to the Development of a Plan for Gradually Ameliorating the Condition of Mankind.* 3d ed. London: Longman, Hurst, Rees, Orme, and Brown, [and others], 1817.

————. *The New Existence of Man upon Earth.* . . . Part III. London: Effingham Wilson, [and others], 1854.

————. *The Life of Robert Owen by Himself.* New York: Alfred A. Knopf, 1920.

————. *A Supplementary Appendix to the First Volume of the Life of Robert Owen.* . . . Vol. I. London: Effingham Wilson, 1858.

Paley, William. *Natural Theology; or, Evidences of the Existence and Attributes of the Deity. Collected from the Appearances of Nature.* New edition. London: W. Mason and Baldwyn and Co., 1817.

Parr, Samuel. *The Works of Samuel Parr.* . . . Edited by J. Johnstone. Vol. II. London: Longman, Rees, Orme, Brown, and Green, 1828.

Place, Francis. *Illustrations and Proofs of the Principle of Population.* . . . Edited by Norman E. Himes. Boston: Houghton Mifflin Company, 1930.

Shelley, Percy Bysshe. *The Complete Works of Percy Bysshe Shelley.* Edited by Roger Ingpen and Walter E. Peck. Vols. I, V, and VII. London: Ernest Benn Limited, 1927-30.

————. *Shelley's Literary and Philosophical Criticism.* Edited by John Shawcross. London: Humphrey Milford, 1932.

Smith, Adam. *An Inquiry into the Nature and Causes of the Wealth of Nations.* Edited by Edwin Cannan. 2 vols. London: Methuen & Co., 1904.

Southey, Charles Cuthbert (ed). *The Life and Correspondence of Robert Southey.* Vols. II and IV. London: Longman, Brown, Green & Longmans, 1850.

Southey, Robert. *Essays, Moral and Political.* London: John Murray, 1832.

Sumner, John Bird. *A Treatise on the Records of the Creation, and on the Moral Attributes of the Creator, with Particular Reference to . . . the Consistency of the Principle of Population with the Wisdom and Goodness of the Deity.* 3d ed. Vol. II. London: J. Hatchard and Son, 1825.

[Wallace, Robert]. *Various Prospects of Mankind, Nature, and Providence.* London: A. Millar, 1761.

Warter, J. W. (ed.). *Selections from the Letters of Robert Southey.* Vol. II. London: Longman, Brown, Green, and Longmans, 1856.

[Weyland, John]. *A Short Inquiry into the Policy, Humanity and Past Effects of the Poor Laws.* . . . London: J. Hatchard, [and others], 1807.

————. *Observations on Mr. Whitbread's Poor Bill, and on the Population of England.* . . . London: J. Hatchard, [and others], 1807.

————. *The Principles of Population and Production.* . . . London: Baldwin, Cradock, and Jay, 1816.

Whitbread, [Samuel]. *Substance of a Speech on the Poor Laws.* . . . London: J. Ridgway, 1807.

Young, Arthur, *The Question of Scarcity Plainly Stated, and Remedies Considered.* . . . London: W. J. and J. Richardson, and J. Wright, 1800.

————. *An Inquiry into the Propriety of Applying Wastes to the Better Maintenance and Support of the Poor.* . . . Bury: Richardsons, and J. Hatchard, 1801.

Periodicals

The Annual Register, 1816, Chronicle.

The Annual Review, II (1803).

The Edinburgh Review, I (October, 1802); XI (October, 1807); XVI (August, 1810); LXIV (January, 1837).

The Quarterly Review, VIII (December, 1812); X (October, 1813); XVI (October, 1816); XVII (July, 1817).

Weekly Political Register, VI (December 8, 1804); VII (February 16, 1805); IX (January 18, 1806); IX (March 14, 1807); XI (May 16, 1807); XI (May 23, 1807); XXXI (August 3, 1816); XXXI (October 5, 1816); XXXI (December 14, 1816).

Weekly Political Register, American edition, XXX (May 18, 1816).

Secondary Sources

Aspinall, Arthur. *Lord Brougham and the Whig Party*. Manchester: The University Press, 1927.

Bonar, James. *Malthus and His Work*. 2d ed. London: George Allen and Unwin Ltd., 1924.

Brinton, Crane. *The Political Ideas of the English Romanticists*. London: Oxford University Press, 1926.

Brown, Ford K. *The Life of William Godwin*. London: J. M. Dent & Sons Ltd., 1926.

Cobban, Alfred. "William Hazlitt," *Encyclopedia of the Social Sciences*. Edited by Edwin R. A. Seligman and Alvin Johnson. Vol. VII, 1932.

Cole, G. D. H. *The Life of William Cobbett*. London: W. Collins Sons and Co., 1927.

————. *The Life of Robert Owen*. 2d ed. London: Macmillan and Company, 1930.

Curry, Kenneth. "A Note on Coleridge's Copy of Malthus," *Publications of the Modern Language Association*, LIV (1939), 613-15.

Fairchild, Henry Pratt. *People. The Quantity and Quality of Population*. New York: Henry Holt and Company, 1939.

Field, James Alfred. *Essays on Population and Other Papers*. Edited by Helen Fisher Hohman. Chicago: The University of Chicago Press, 1931.

Gini, Corrado, *et al. Population. Lectures on the Harris Foundation, 1929*. Chicago: The University of Chicago Press, 1930.

Griffith, G. Talbot. *Population Problems in the Age of Malthus*. Cambridge, England: The University Press, 1926.

Halévy, Élie. *A History of the English People in 1815*. New York: Harcourt, Brace and Co., 1924.

————. *A History of the English People, 1830-1841*. Translated by F. I. Watkins. New York: Harcourt, Brace & Co., n. d.

Hammond, J. L. and Barbara. *The Village Labourer, 1760-1832. A Study in the Government of England before the Reform Bill*. 4th ed. London: Longmans, Green, and Co. Ltd., 1927.

————. *The Town Labourer, 1760-1832. The New Civilization*. London: Longmans, Green and Co. Ltd., 1928.

Howe, P. P. *The Life of William Hazlitt*. New York: Richard R. Smith, Inc., 1930.

McCulloch, J. R. *A Statistical Account of the British Empire*. London: C. Knight and Company, 1837.

Maclean, Catherine Macdonald. *Born Under Saturn. A Biography of William Hazlitt*. New York: The Macmillan Company, 1944.

Nicholls, Sir George: *A History of the English Poor Laws.* 2 vols. London: John Murray, 1854.

Nicholson, J. S. *The History of the English Corn Laws.* London: Swan Sonnenschein and Co., 1904.

Paul, C. Kegan. *William Godwin, His Friends and Contemporaries.* Vol. I. London: Henry S. King & Co., 1876.

Potter, George Reuben. "Unpublished Marginalia in Coleridge's Copy of Malthus's Essay on Population," *Publications of the Modern Language Association,* LI (1936), 1061-68.

Report of the Royal Commission on Poor Laws and Relief of Distress. London: His Majesty's Stationery Office, 1909.

Reuter, Edward B. *Population Problems.* 2d ed. rev. Chicago: J. B. Lippincott Company, 1937.

Smart, William. *Economic Annals of the Nineteenth Century.* Vol. I. London: Macmillan and Co., 1910.

Thompson, Warren S. *Population Problems.* 2d ed. New York: McGraw-Hill Book Company, Inc., 1935.

Trevelyan, George Macaulay. *British History in the Nineteenth Century, 1782-1901.* London: Longmans, Green, and Co., 1934.

Wallas, Graham. *The Life of Francis Place.* 4th ed. London: George Allen & Unwin Ltd., 1925.

West, Julius. *A History of the Chartist Movement.* London: Constable and Co., 1920.

Woods, George B., Watt, Homer A., and Anderson, George K. *The Literature of England.* 3d ed. Vol. II. Chicago: Scott, Foresman and Company, 1948.

Williston, Horace. "Hazlitt as a Critic of the 'Modern Philosophy.'" Unpublished Ph.D. dissertation, Dept. of English, University of Chicago, 1938.

Young, G. M. (ed.). *Early Victorian England 1830-1865.* Vol. I. London: Oxford University Press, Humphry Milford, 1934.

Zimmerman, Carle C. *Consumption and Standards of Living.* New York: D. Van Nostrand Company, Inc., 1936.

INDEX